ALAN SHEARER'S DIARY OF A SEASON

Written in collaboration with
Dave Harrison

First published in Great Britain in 1995 by
Virgin Books
an imprint of Virgin Publishing Ltd
332 Ladbroke Grove
London W10 5AH

A catalogue record for this book is available from the British Library

ISBN 1 85227 590 1

Typeset by TW Typesetting, Plymouth, Devon
Printed and bound in Great Britain by
Mackays of Chatham, Lordswood, Chatham, Kent

CONTENTS

FOREWORD

David Platt

Alan Shearer has the potential to be talked about in the same breath as the great Dutch striker Marco van Basten.

His all-round centre forward ability identifies him already as one of the best in the world and if he continues to be receptive to the different progressive methods and tactics of football, he will undoubtedly continue to improve even further.

His manager, Kenny Dalglish, was once quoted as saying, 'What else can you say about Alan Shearer?' I can sympathise with his problem. Indeed, the esteem in which he is held by managers, players, journalists and fans makes it difficult to comprehend that he is only 24 years old.

His performances belie his age, as does his manner off the pitch. His success has brought him fame and with fame has come the glory; but glory and fame also bring pressure. It is the way he has taken everything in his stride that is truly commendable. He has accepted the pressure and used it as a tool for his own advantage. This trait lifts him to the stratosphere of being more than just a footballer.

When Dalglish paid £3.3m to Southampton for Alan Shearer's services, people looked and wondered. Alan scored on his debut and has found the net since with a consistency that, for a goal-scorer like myself, is almost annoying but at the same time highly admirable. His goals have helped Blackburn win the Premiership for the first time in 81 years. While he would be the first to say that his team-mates deserve the credit for his goals and the success the club has achieved, quite simply, without

Alan in the side they would not have won the title. *He* makes the difference.

David Platt
May 1995

INTRODUCTION

It is approaching five in the morning on Monday, 15th May 1995, and it is deadly quiet. After fifteen or so crazy hours of noise and frenzied celebration, the silence is very welcome. I am sitting at home and taking a long, lingering look at my Premiership medal – the first major honour I have won in my career. I have not seen much of this glittering prize since it was presented to me on the pitch at Anfield eleven hours ago. It has been hidden away in the baby's nappy bag, placed there for safe-keeping by my wife Lainya before we joined the biggest party Blackburn Rovers have had for 81 years. The medal is going to take pride of place in my trophy display soon but for the moment I want to hold on to it and recall the highs and lows of a year in my life that I will never forget.

Earlier, I popped in to see our children Chloe, aged two, and Hollie, five months, both sound asleep, totally unaware of the drama which has just unfolded. My wife and daughters have kept me sane over these last few months and provided me with a shelter from the tension which, at times, became almost unbearable. I am lucky that my home life offers me an escape from the so-called pressures of football and, in turn, I try to protect them from the mood swings brought on by the triumphs and failures every player has to endure. It has not always been easy. Football is a game of extremes and during the past year my emotions have been stretched over the full range. But it has been worth it. Every single minute. And I have this medal to display alongside the awards I have received – Professional Footballers'

Association Player of the Year, Blackburn Rovers Supporters' Players of the Year and the Golden Boot for being top goal-scorer in the Premiership. The Championship tops everything else because it is the first honour I have won as part of a team and I have considered it a privilege to be a member of this Blackburn side. It has been a genuine collective effort. When the stick was flying – and there has been plenty of that from people jealous of our resources and success – we have closed ranks and got on with the job. We have been accused of lacking flair and not showing the true style of champions, whatever that means. But I heard someone say at the end of the season that the League table never lies and we will settle for that theory. The final figures show we collected more points and scored more goals than anyone else and, in my view, that means we are a team that provides results and entertainment. This title was won by a group of men who are treated as equals; in a dressing-room where there are no stars and no cliques. These are the players with whom I have worked, played and shared the finest moment of my career:

Tim Flowers: I have never seen a more complete goalkeeping performance than the one he produced in the 1-0 victory over Newcastle in our last but one game of the season. Known as 'Cat', he loves a laugh and a joke but few players work harder than he does. If you ring him at home, he will answer the phone by saying 'Safest hands in soccer' or 'England's No. 1'. This is his way of taking the mickey out of himself but he believes he is the best and so do we.

Bobby Mimms: He has spent most of the season on the bench as substitute goalkeeper but when his chance eventually came, he did not let us down. He stood in for Tim when he was out with a broken toe and suspension and made an incredible save when he pushed a shot from Gary McAllister on to the post to earn us a 1-1 draw against Leeds. Wherever he goes his sidekick Mark Atkins is never far away and we call them Danny and Arnie.

Henning Berg: He is amazingly consistent and I don't remember him having a bad game all season. He also showed his versatility by switching from full back to centre back when needed. I put him in the same 'Mr Dependable' category as Manchester United's Denis Irwin. He takes a lot of stick from the other lads because he is Norwegian but his answer is to point to his country's World Cup record in recent years and that shuts everyone up.

Jeff Kenna: He only played nine games at the end of the season after joining us from Southampton but the club has given him a medal for the part he played. He deserves it too. He came into the side like a breath of fresh air and played in four different positions, scoring a goal in that important 2-1 over Crystal Palace, four games from the finish. He started to grow a moustache in the final few weeks of the campaign and it earned him the nickname Freddie Mercury. It soon came off.

Graeme Le Saux: He has made the England left back position his own over the last couple of seasons with his performances for his club and country. No one appreciates the accuracy of his crosses from the left more than me because he has created many of my goals. He is considered a bit of an intellectual because he reads the *Guardian* and has an interest in antiques – but no one holds that against him.

Alan Wright: After playing a handful of games for us at full back and on the left side of midfield, he left us to join Aston Villa and nearly enjoyed playing for a Championship side and relegated team in the same season. Very small but very skilful, he answers to the nickname 'Dwarf'.

Tony Gale: At the start of the season he was struggling to find himself a club. I think Barnet was his best hope until our assistant manager, Ray Harford, asked him to play in a friendly against Celtic because we were so short of players through injury. He ended up playing a significant role in the centre of our defence at the start of the season and, at 36, is now the proud owner of a Championship medal. He provided us with an old, experienced head when we needed it. He also gave us quite a few dodgy racing tips. He didn't get one right all season which didn't worry him because he didn't back them himself.

Colin Hendry: This has been the best season of his life. There can be no braver footballer in the game. I can still see him when we were hanging on for victory at Everton, throwing his head and body into the thick of the action to defend our goal. Nobody is more willing to work for the club's cause than Colin and if there is a Supporters' Club event or charity presentation going on, he will be there. He is known as the 'Blond Bombshell', though we suspect he gets his hair colour from a bottle.

Ian Pearce: He was signed from Chelsea for £200,000 when no one was quite sure whether he was a defender or a striker. He has claimed one of the central defensive positions with his strength in the air and on the ground. He is only 21 but plays as though he is 31 and you would think he had been in the Premiership all his life. I have started to call him Eric because I think he resembles Cantona – though only in looks.

Tim Sherwood: I have been at Blackburn for three years now and in that time Tim has just got better and better. He does all the good things expected from a midfield player – tackles, passes, scores goals and gets up and down the pitch. He has fully deserved his England recognition. He's a cockney and a bit of a Jack the Lad. He has an amazing head of long hair but when I give him some stick about it, he replies, 'At least I've got some – not like you.'

Mark Atkins: He has filled David Batty's boots for most of the season and done a terrific job. He weighed in with some valuable goals, most notably in the 3-2 victory over Liverpool at Ewood Park. He is strong and mobile and is known as 'Arrow'.

Paul Warhurst: He is incredibly versatile. Whenever there is a problem position – defence, midfield or up front – he can fill it, though his luck with injuries has been cruel. When he joined us from Sheffield Wednesday he brought with him the nickname 'Albert Tatlock'. I don't know why but I suppose he does sound as if he has just walked in from the set of *Coronation Street.*

David Batty: With him in our team all season, the title race would probably have been over a month before it was finally decided. A foot injury restricted him to just four full appearances and although the club wanted to give him a Championship medal, he turned it down because he didn't think he had earned one. That's typical of 'Bats' – he is a bulldog of a competitor but has more skill than he is given credit for.

Stuart Ripley: Did not score all season but his supply from the right wing has been invaluable and so has his non-stop work rate. In our system the wide players are vitally important and he fits the bill perfectly. He is another intellectual who reads the *Independent* and does crosswords. He also has a degree in French. It's a pity his English is not a bit better because he comes from Middlesbrough and few people can understand him.

Jason Wilcox: The biggest compliment I can pay him is that when he was ruled out for the run-in to the title, we missed him enormously. He gives us width and balance down the left and provides the sort of crosses any striker will thrive on. We call him 'The Stick' because he is so skinny but he is deceptively strong, fast and very fit.

Kevin Gallacher: His season lasted about 67 minutes but in that time he scored a very important goal to help us beat Crystal Palace before being carried off with a leg fracture. He had worked so hard to recover from a similar injury only to see his efforts go to waste but his small contribution was gratefully received. He is not very big and is Scottish, so he is known as 'The Moose'.

Robbie Slater: He is a bundle of energy who has filled in on the right and left side of midfield and always makes his presence felt with his work rate and energy. He has played in France, calls himself an Australian and has played for their national team, yet comes from Ormskirk, just down the road from where I live. Work that one out. He is called 'The Lobster' because he has a red face and red hair.

Chris Sutton: If you had told him before the start of the season he would finish with 21 goals after his £5m move from Norwich, he would have been delighted. He was disappointed the goals did not flow so regularly in the second half of the campaign but he still gave his all and was a major contributor to our success. He handled his big move wonderfully well and is popular in the dressing-room. He earned the nickname 'Trigger' when he first joined us but when we are feeling generous towards him we call him 'Sooty'.

Mike Newell: He has had almost a permanent place on the bench since recovering from his knee injury but when called upon as substitute he has come into the side and steadied things by keeping hold of the ball in tight situations. Another great lad to have around for team spirit, he is known as 'Mr Angry' because he has a short fuse. He would argue black is white!

Alan Shearer: I was known as 'Shocks' in my Southampton days, though I have not got a clue why. Since my move to Blackburn a few have started calling me 'Billy Big Pockets'. That nickname was given to me by our groundsman at Ewood Park, Steve Patrick, after he read in a newspaper what I was supposed to be earning each week.

More seriously, it has been a thrill to play my part in a Championship team, scoring 34 League goals, which equals the record total for a season in the Premiership. But, in addition to my goals total, I am immensely proud of the fact that I was the only member of the squad to play in all 42 League games. It is worth remembering that before the start of the season people were wondering whether I would ever be the same player after rumours were spread that I was suffering from a serious illness.

There have been times when I have played with injuries and others when I have turned out after having pain-killing injections but it has never been an ordeal to figure in the most exciting Championship race for years. Admittedly we could have sewn it up long before the final day but our dip in form at the end was probably due to our lack of experience. Do not forget that this was only our third season back in the top flight and never before have we led from the front and put ourselves in a position to be shot at. We will benefit from this fight to the finish and be better equipped in years to come.

When the dust has settled on this memorable campaign, the future will open up ahead of Blackburn Rovers and there will be no limit to the club's ambitions. Jack Walker has not spent £60m just to win one title. He wants more success, more trophies and he wants to conquer Europe. He will make sure the club does not stand still and there will be comings and goings, just as there have been in years gone by. People constantly ask me where I figure in all this. I have had to live with speculation for as long as I can remember about me moving here, there and everywhere. Italy seems to be the most popular destination but not once have I said I want to leave Blackburn. My future will take care of itself. I am a great believer in fate and, if I am destined to move to Italy one day, then so be it. But whatever happens, there will never be another season quite like the one which has just ended.

ACKNOWLEDGEMENTS

My thanks to the trustworthy Dave Harrison for putting down my words in such an accurate and readable manner.

Thanks also to Michael Preston for helping compile the statistics, with assistance from Peter White of the *Lancashire Evening Telegraph* who have also provided many of the photographs.

Thanks to Lainya, Chloe and Hollie for their love and consistency during my year of ups and downs.

And thanks to everyone at Blackburn – players and officials alike – for helping me experience a season I will never forget.

Alan Shearer

ILLUSTRATIONS

DIARY OF A SEASON 1994–95

JULY 1994

After a short break from football I always find myself looking forward to the coming season – I feel more eager this year than ever before because of Blackburn's fine finish to the 1993/94 season.

MONDAY 11TH

I travel to the Gleneagles Golf and Country Club in Perthshire with my wife Lainya, team-mate Mike Newell and his wife Catherine for a few days of golf and relaxation without our children. It's a beautiful place – not just for the golf courses but the hotel facilities which include sauna, swimming pool, etc. We manage four rounds of golf in the three days and I come out on top 3-1. I'm a 16-handicapper and play as often as possible, living as I do near to courses at Formby and Birkdale.

I first began to swing a golf club when I was a young kid in Newcastle but it was far removed from the manicured fairways and greens and splendour of Gleneagles. I bought a couple of clubs in a jumble sale and would play on a field near my home. I never had any proper tuition – I would just put the ball down and smack it as far as I could. Sometimes me and a few mates would sneak into the Newcastle City Golf Club just before dark when everyone had finished their rounds and play a few holes. That was a big thrill for us lads from the local council estate.

When I was an apprentice professional at Southampton I bought my first proper set of clubs and began to take it more seriously. People tell me I have a terrible swing, but I usually manage to hit the ball straight and a fair distance. I enjoy the challenge of golf but I get as much pleasure out of the game as a form of relaxation. There is nothing more refreshing than being in the open spaces on a fine day – away from the noise of ringing telephones and heavy traffic.

TUESDAY 12TH

A phone call to my parents reveals that the *Sun* is carrying a story claiming I am bound for Italy because of Chris Sutton's impending move to Blackburn from Norwich. It's true that I have contemplated playing in Italy – but not just yet. I have two years left on my contract and I intend to see them out. I want to win honours with Blackburn and enjoy a successful European Championship with England in 1996. Only then will I assess my future plans.

If I do go to Italy – and it's not a foregone conclusion – there can be no better example to follow than my England room-mate David Platt. He began to learn the language well in advance and was quickly able to adjust to the culture. Now he almost regards himself as an Italian – he speaks, dresses, eats and conducts his whole lifestyle as one.

Like any player I want to aim for the top and Italian football does seem to lure most of the world's best players and arouse terrific passion and excitement. The financial rewards are quite attractive too . . .

Along with the rest of the nation I was absolutely transfixed by the World Cup in 1990. I was back at my family home in Newcastle and was glued to the television for virtually every match. The atmosphere was electric and the stadia fantastic. It crossed my mind even then that I would love to be part of that scene every week but I never dreamed that, four years later, I would start to be the subject of endless speculation about moving to one of the big Serie A clubs.

I plan to take Italian lessons later this year. Even if I don't end up there, it will be a useful learning exercise – and will come in handy for ordering pizzas.

Meanwhile I have to live with all the speculation about my future. I'm sure it won't go away.

FRIDAY 15TH

I am doing a photo shoot for Umbro at Manchester City's training ground when I discover Chris Sutton has signed for Blackburn for £5 million. Another good player joins the club. There'll be terrific competition with myself, Kevin Gallacher, Mike Newell and Paul Warhurst all vying for places up front. Chris will soon realise that a big money transfer won't guarantee him anything at Ewood Park!

There's going to be pressure on Chris because of the size of the fee – a new British record. He has already said that no one's worth that much money, much the same as I did when I moved from Southampton for £3.3 million. But like me Chris has to push that out of his mind and accept that the transfer valuation has nothing to do with him – then get on with his football. He'll get abusive letters and chants from the terraces of 'What a waste of money' just like I did, but he has to be strong enough to handle it.

My postbag at the time of my transfer was quite unnerving. Some of the messages were plain pathetic – 'You have made a big mistake signing for Blackburn and you will pay for it', 'You have just gone there for the money. Blackburn will never win anything.' Others were more sinister and made threats to my mum, dad and wife. After the initial shock I just laughed them off, screwed them into a ball and threw them into the dustbin.

I think I played against Chris when he made his debut for Norwich as a tall, gangling centre half. I think he's a better striker – good in the air, holds the ball up well, scores goals. What more could you ask?

SUNDAY 17TH

The day starts well with the news that Abbie Humphries, the baby who has been missing for fifteen days, is found safe and well. As parents of a 21-month-old daughter Chloe and with another child on the way, we shared the anguish suffered by

Abbie's parents but spared thoughts too for the poor girl who was desperate enough to want to steal someone else's baby.

It's a big day on the sporting calendar, with the final round of the Open Golf Championship and the World Cup Final. We're having a barbecue for friends but I keep being drawn to the television for the final few holes of the golf. Mike Newell is on the phone telling me that he has £50 on Jesper Parnevik to win the title at 7-1. The Swede blows it on the final hole and the cameras capture his despair as Nick Price grabs the glory and the trophy. I bet Mike Newell feels as bad as Parnevik. Total dejection too for Italy's Roberto Baggio after missing the penalty which gives Brazil the World Cup. Not a classic final but a dramatic finish – I think the trophy went to the team with the most flair and the outstanding individuals.

My heart goes out to Baggio, though. I've been in a penalty shoot-out and appreciate the agony he was suffering. Three seasons ago Southampton won the first FA Cup tie to be decided by a shoot-out against Manchester United. There were 30,000 Mancunians baying for my blood.

I scored in front of the Stretford End and since then I have never been the most popular player to visit Old Trafford. Even though I converted my penalty that day, I do not think it is a very satisfactory way of deciding important matches, though no one has yet come up with a better method. A miss from the spot must haunt a player for a long time and could have a detrimental effect on his career. When Stuart Pearce and Chris Waddle failed to score in the shoot-out against Germany in the 1990 World Cup semi-finals, I knew they would have to live with that for the rest of their lives. Fortunately both of them were strong enough characters to overcome the setbacks and continue their careers successfully.

All the way through the World Cup I can't help thinking that England should have been there and believe we would have given a good account of ourselves. I console myself with the thought that I am young enough to be in with a chance of making the finals in 1998 – fitness and form permitting.

But it would still have been the thrill of a lifetime to perform in the United States in front of packed houses and a worldwide TV audience. Our attempt at qualification was written off as an unmitigated disaster and Graham Taylor was pilloried more than any other England manager I can remember. But how many people recall that he was without me, Stuart Pearce and Paul Gascoigne for a significant part of the campaign?

With everyone fit I believe we would have booked our tickets for the finals but you need luck at times in international football and Graham did not always enjoy it.

MONDAY 18TH

Back to work. Near neighbours Mike Newell, Tim Flowers and I share a lift for the first day's training which we approach with some trepidation. I was particularly lazy during the first part of the summer and only began some voluntary runs over the last couple of weeks. I know it's going to be painful when the hard slog of building basic fitness begins.

I finish third from last in the run around six laps of a school playing-field, first in the 30 metres sprint and third in the 100 metres. I guess that tells you what my strength is as an athlete but Linford Christie has nothing to fear.

Chris Sutton settles in quietly and is lucky to escape without any of the usual pranks dished out to new boys. We haven't even thought of a nickname for him yet. But Chris will already have found out there is no room for big-shots at Blackburn. Everyone is treated the same, no matter how much they cost. Kenny Dalglish makes sure of that. No one has achieved more than him in football but he mucks in with the lads and has a laugh and a joke, without ever forgetting to remind us who's boss.

No sign of him yet, though. He's staying on holiday for another week. He'll be back when the balls come out and all the hard work is over.

TUESDAY 19TH

There's a lot of police activity at Ewood Park because a dead body's been found during the digging operations on the site of a new grandstand. Is this the first casualty of pre-season training? Could it be the boss whom we haven't seen for ages? Actually, the first casualty is me. During a four-mile run we have to negotiate a one-and-a-half hill climb on uneven concrete. The jarring causes my back to go into spasm. It's the same problem I had briefly last season when it went during a match against QPR and forced me to miss an England International.

This isn't so serious but still depresses me and requires a few days' rest. In a bad mood, I ask Mike Newell to bring his car right up to the dressing-room door for a quick getaway.

A man approaches me and says he has driven 180 miles to get a picture of me with his daughter. She jumps in the car and gets a quick photo and an autograph, but the *Daily Mail* reporter who wants an interview is politely told to come back next week.

But as we drive away I turn and notice the man with the young girl, shaking his head at the abrupt treatment he has received. I feel really guilty. I know how dedicated these supporters are and try to devote as much attention as I can to them. This time they caught me on a bad day.

FRIDAY 22ND

Alex Ferguson is quoted in the newspapers as saying Blackburn Rovers are wrecking the transfer market with signings like the £5 million Sutton deal. Obviously such moves have an inflationary effect but there is another way of looking at it.

Our owner Jack Walker is buying players from his own personal resources, which means money is being pumped into the game which otherwise wouldn't have been there. That must be good for football. Jack Walker worked hard to build up his fortune, starting from the very bottom, so surely he has a right to decide how to spend it. He is a down-to-earth type without any airs and graces and loves his football club. How can anyone knock him for wanting the best for Rovers?

WEDNESDAY 27TH

A long hard run for 38 minutes, alternating between jogging, sprinting and half and three-quarter pace running. I am lagging at the back and don't feel right. I am never among the frontrunners in these sort of training stints but I have never felt like this before. I cannot push myself and feel lifeless and lethargic. I finish in a cold sweat and know there must be something seriously wrong with me. I decide it's best to see a doctor as we're leaving for a pre-season trip to Norway on Friday.

THURSDAY 28TH

After a hard session with the ball, Jack Walker invites us all to the Fernhurst Hotel near to the ground, where food and drinks are laid on. He welcomes all the newcomers and wishes us all the best for the new season.

I don't fancy anything to eat and feel under the weather. On the way home I ring my wife to ask her to arrange for me to see a doctor. She's not in but when she returns we manage to get the last appointment at 6.00 p.m. He tells me I've picked up a virus, probably from eating seafood when I was on holiday in Portugal in June. I have been tired and lifeless but put that down to the effects of training. Now the doc tells me it would be unwise to go to Norway and that I need blood tests. I ring the boss and he agrees it would be wrong to go against medical advice.

Not the ideal pre-season start for me but it was similar last season when I was getting over my knee operation. I managed to catch up then by putting in extra work during the afternoons, so I'll do the same again this time.

SATURDAY 30TH

I spend most of my time at home watching TV, still feeling pretty grotty. I tune into the horse-racing. I'm not an avid fan and very rarely have a bet but while I was at the Lilleshall rehabilitation centre last year I got friendly with the jockey Brendan Powell. He took me to one or two meetings where I became familiar with the hazards of life in the saddle and falling off a horse at speeds of up to 40 mph. That was brought home to me a day or two ago when Lester Piggott survived a horrific tumble. He's 58 years old and still going strong. That's even older than Kevin Moran, but I reckon our veteran defender has broken more bones than your average jockey.

Tim Flowers, who's on the injured list after ripping open his arm on a net peg in training, rings from Norway to tell me we lost 2-1 to Steinkjaer. The game was played on a rock-hard pitch with no grass and the sun beating down. Its only real benefit was as a fitness exercise.

SUNDAY 31ST

The Sunday papers have a bit of a go at Chris Sutton, claiming he was unimpressive on his debut. Talk about instant judgement. I know how he feels. We lost 3-0 to Hibs on my debut. I really wanted to impress in my first appearance in a Rovers shirt but pre-season friendlies are not the games to set the world alight. All eyes were on me and I was expected to look a £3.3m player from the word go. It was an impossible task but try telling the Press that. Chris was on a hiding to nothing as well. If he'd scored a hat-trick they would have said he should have scored four.

I manage to venture out of the house to turn the sprinkler on the lawn and then on to the local garden centre with Chloe to see the ducks. I feel slightly better but still not on top of the world.

AUGUST 1994

MONDAY 1ST

Another doctor's appointment brings confirmation that the virus was caused by eating seafood. The cure is to do absolutely nothing for a week to ten days. I've lost about a stone in weight but am slowly getting my appetite back. I love pasta and my wife's an excellent cook, so it's been strange for me to have so little to eat.

TUESDAY 2ND

I hear the lads have won the second match of the pre-season tour 6-1. Again no significance is attached to the result, though I gather from my on-the-spot reporter Tim Flowers that the team performance was much better.

I'm really missing not being with the lads now – and not only because it's such a crucial part of our preparation for the new season.

We're having a new kitchen and utility room built and the whole house is a mess. I love having things neat and tidy so I had arranged for the work to be done while I was away on tour. Fortunately, the weather is good and I can escape to the garden for some peace and quiet.

WEDNESDAY 3RD

I can't stand the thought of another six days stuck at home, so I take our Golden Retriever Candy for a walk along the beach for three hours. It is good to get some fresh air and I feel much better for the exercise, even though it's just a gentle stroll.

I can spend hours alone on these walks and find them as invigorating and relaxing as my rounds of golf. I disappear among the sand dunes just a stone's throw from my home and enjoy the isolation. Occasionally I will bump into someone but the only conversation is a friendly 'hello'. No one wants to stop and talk about football.

Candy enjoys the freedom and exercise just as much as when she was a puppy. Lainya handed her to me in a cardboard box as a nineteenth birthday present. My wife was not too keen on having a dog at first, having suffered the horror of seeing her family pet run over. I had grown up with a dog in my house and Lainya eventually gave in and agreed we should have one of our own.

THURSDAY 4TH

More tests. The doctor reports 40 per cent improvement in my condition from the original diagnosis. However, he stresses how important it is not to rush things and tells me I won't be fit for the Charity Shield on August 14th and will probably miss the first two to three weeks of the season. The newspapers are still having a field day, speculating on the seriousness of my illness. I try to explain to reporters what the position is. Some print what I tell them. Others appear not to believe me and write what they think is the best version.

My parents return from holiday in Greece and I chat to them on the phone and tell them not to believe all the scare stories they've seen in the papers.

FRIDAY 5TH

I ring the doctor for the latest test results and my recovery is still on course. I also speak to the gaffer as the team are on the way up to Scotland for two friendlies. I tell him I've made plans to travel to Southampton for Lainya's cousin Rebecca's wedding. The boss is still happy to leave things in my hands.

The journey to Southampton is horrendous. It normally takes three and three-quarter hours by car, but it takes over five hours in baking heat. The baby is crying and the dog is gasping for breath and it's such a relief to get there.

Southampton is full of fond memories for me and we will probably settle there again when I finish my playing career. I went to live down on the south coast as a fifteen year old straight from school and joined the football club as an apprentice professional.

It was not easy at first. I felt homesick and missed my family, but it was to turn into a great adventure which I wouldn't have missed for the world. I lived in digs and was lucky enough to be looked after by Maureen and Nigel Wareham who welcomed me into their home like an adopted son.

I was fortunate, too, to have Neil Maddison alongside me. He was a fellow Geordie who joined the Saints on the same day as me and we forged a friendship which is still as strong today.

Lainya misses her family and friends and likes to return home whenever possible. But she knew when she married a footballer that at any time she might have to move to another part of the country and she does not complain.

SATURDAY 6TH

The wedding goes well. I am on a strict no-alcohol diet but I do sneak a sip of champagne to toast the bride.

Rovers lose 1-0 to Aberdeen but it was a fairly makeshift side with Chris Sutton, Mike Newell, Kevin Gallacher, Paul Warhurst, Jason Wilcox and David Batty all on the casualty list. Kenny Dalglish and coach Tony Parkes are pressed into action. I bet it was a struggle for anyone to get a pass from the gaffer whenever he had the ball. He still behaves like a player and I am unlucky enough to be in his team in our eight-a-side games in training. If you pass him the ball there is a 99 per cent chance you will never get it back. But, seriously, you can see why he was such a special player. He was one of my heroes when I was a young lad. I remember my Uncle Dave taking me to see Liverpool play against Bury in the FA Cup and I was the envy of all my mates to be able to watch the all-conquering Pool from the famous Kop. I could not take my eyes off Dalglish and marvelled at the way he combined with Ian Rush. One of the things which stood out was his backside! He has this enormous behind which he would use to shield the ball from defenders. It is still just as big and he uses it to good effect in our training matches.

My first club manager at Southampton, Chris Nicholl, often told me to 'Stick your bum out like Dalglish' and I knew exactly what he meant. When I joined Blackburn from the Saints, the chance of working with Kenny Dalglish was a major factor influencing my decision. I had studied the master from a distance and the chance to learn from him first-hand could not be missed.

MONDAY 8TH

The journey back from Southampton is a lot quicker. I have to pick up a letter from my own doctor to give to the club doctor. I've become a Teletext addict and flick through the pages to learn that we have lost 1-0 to Celtic. We've still got a long list of injuries, and youngsters Peter Thorne and Ian Pearce were called into the squad. Our performance was apparently quite good and we missed several chances in a close game.

TUESDAY 9TH

I go into the club for the first time in two weeks to see Dr Burke, the club doctor. He takes some more tests and seems satisfied with my improvement. Back home, the days drag on very slowly. The kitchen is still in a mess and I'm struggling to occupy all my spare time. Someone once remarked that for such a hard-working player, I'm incredibly lazy off the pitch. Well, all this lazing around is driving me mad. Physically I feel great now. I've put all my lost weight back on and am, in fact, a pound heavier than I should be. That won't be a problem once I start training again. I'm one of those lucky people who can eat virtually anything and not pile on the pounds.

WEDNESDAY 10TH

Some unexpected but really good news today. I pop into the club offices to check on my post and the chairman Robert Coar asks to see me. The club want to give me an amended contract and a new pay deal with no extension to the length of it. It's a marvellous gesture which has come completely out of the blue. I signed a couple of new deals at Southampton and there were always strings attached. There are none this time. I did not ask for a wage rise, so I guess Rovers must be reasonably satisfied with what I'm doing.

Later I do a television commercial for the *News of the World*. I've signed up with them to write ten articles over the season. The filming goes a lot more smoothly than usual and I'm back home at 5 o'clock. I tell Lainya about my discussion with the chairman. We both know how lucky I am to be at a club like Blackburn.

THURSDAY 11TH

I pop into the ground to do a bit of training – a few light weights to build up my hamstrings. I'm sitting in my car waiting to give Tim Flowers a lift home when all hell breaks loose. Several journalists have got hold of my car phone number and in turn they ring me to ask if it's true that I've got hepatitis. Since being taken ill, I've heard rumours that I've had everything from tuberculosis to leukaemia. I'm expecting to hear that I've got Aids soon.

But hepatitis seems to be the popular diagnosis now. That's the complaint which Gary Lineker had many years ago. Jimmy Greaves also went down with it, so the opinions of these two are canvassed, with the conclusion that I might never be the same player again. We'll see.

I try to explain to everyone that it is not anywhere near so serious. Again, some pressmen believe me, some don't. I'm not really bothered because I know I'm close to a full recovery. The answerphone is switched on at home and stays on all night. Another nine journalists ring and leave messages.

It is part and parcel of a footballer's job to deal with the Press but I think, without exception, most players exercise extreme caution. I remember being warned when I first came into the game to be very suspicious of reporters. I heard so many scare stories about colleagues being misquoted and misinterpreted and the instinctive reaction was to keep the media at arm's length. After a while, you learn which ones to trust and which to avoid. I believe I have a good working relationship with the majority of them and I find that if you are willing to afford them a reasonable amount of time and co-operation, then you get a favourable response.

FRIDAY 12TH

My first job is to have a new telephone line put in with a new number. I wonder how long it will be before the Press get hold of it. Still, I suppose that's part of their job. I arrange for four tickets for the Charity Shield for employees of my car sponsors Lex Rover and I do some more light training – just gentle exercise with a few weights. The buzz is building around Ewood Park with Sunday's Charity Shield at Wembley against Manchester United approaching fast. We're still carrying a lot of injuries and I estimate that there'll be about £17 million worth of players sitting on the sidelines – Mike Newell, Kevin Gallacher, David Batty, Chris Sutton and myself.

SATURDAY 13TH

My 24th birthday. Chloe allows me my first birthday treat by letting me lie in bed till 9 o'clock. I get up and open my presents. Lainya has bought me a new stack stereo system. I like listening to Phil Collins and Rod Stewart and always have the radio on for the latest sports news. The club has delivered hundreds of cards which were sent to the ground – a mixture of birthday and get well cards.

Because I'm not in the squad for the Charity Shield, I'm able to spend half a day with Lainya and Chloe on my birthday, which is nice. Mike Newell and I have arranged to meet the team bus at an M6 service station to travel down to London with them. It's great to be back among the lads again. All the usual banter is flying around, though I'm amazed there is no practical joke waiting for me. They must be feeling sorry for me.

I tackle skipper Tim Sherwood about an article in one of the papers in which he said, 'There are no superstars at Blackburn. Well, maybe one – Alan Shearer. We were all disappointed when he didn't get the part of James Bond when it was up for grabs recently.' He looks embarrassed when I bring it up, but I know it was only a bit of harmless fun.

SUNDAY 14TH

A real lie-in. I rise at 10.30 a.m., read the newspapers and join the lads on the morning of the game. Mike and I have been invited to have lunch at the Wembley conference centre and a car is sent to collect us. Afterwards, we ask a security guard to show us through the back corridors of the conference centre to get to the stadium and avoid having to fight our way through the crowds. However, we still have to go across a car park to get to the players' entrance and inevitably we are recognised.

A chant of 'There's only one Alan Shearer' goes up, when suddenly a United fan thrusts his face into mine and says, 'You're an effin' user and a greedy so-and-so.' (I told you I was popular among Mancunians.) Before I realise what is happening, a Blackburn fan bops him one and leaves him flat on his back. We are glad to get to the safety of the dressing-rooms.

There is cheering and counter-cheering as all of us injured players make our way around the pitch to watch the game. We lose 2-0 to goals from Eric Cantona and Paul Ince but in the circumstances we give a good account of ourselves. I would rather lose this game and pick up three points next Saturday.

This is the first evidence I have seen of the so-called referees' clampdown, which is a follow-on from the strict application of the rules brought in during the World Cup. In my view there's no need for it. There's nothing wrong with our game, so why change it? One of the great attractions of British football is its speed and aggression. It's a man's game and all of us are prepared to give and take a few knocks. Take that competitive edge away and you'll spoil it. There are seven bookings at Wembley and one of those cautioned is Ryan Giggs. That says it all about the new get-tough approach. But I am sure things will settle down, just as they did in the World Cup, and referees will use their own judgement and common sense.

I see Terry Venables in the players' lounge at Wembley and he asks me how I'm feeling. He has obviously read some of the reports about me being on my deathbed, so I'm happy to reassure him that I'm alive and well and will hopefully be playing again soon.

I also have a chat with Jack Walker after the game and we discuss whether I will be match fit for the opening Premiership game against my old club Southampton next Saturday. Jack is right when he says, 'Patience is a virtue, lad. No point in rushing back to play on Saturday and setting yourself back for another few weeks.'

We arrive back at the motorway services at 11.00 p.m. and I give Tim and Mike a lift home. We stop off at a drive-through McDonalds for a late-night feast and I get to bed at 12.20 a.m. It's all right for the other two – they've got a day off tomorrow.

MONDAY 15TH

I don't mind getting up early. This is my first day back in real training. Physio Mike Pettigrew suggests I join in some light jogging but we get a bit carried away and it feels like half a marathon. It's great to get a sweat on again after three weeks of doing next to nothing. I drive home, tired but on top of the world. I feel like a human being again.

Lainya's mum and dad travel up to see us. They've bought a new Barbour jacket for me for my birthday present, ideal for taking the dog out for long walks in the winter.

TUESDAY 16TH

I feel no after-effects from the previous day and join the rest of the players for the annual photo call. Like most photo calls, it drags on and doesn't finish till midday.

I can't wait to get out to training with our fitness coach, Eddie Baronowski. He usually comes in twice a week when there are no midweek games, to put us through our paces. I come through the sprint work better than I expected and then a longer, harder running session. I had ten days' work under my belt before the illness struck but I reckon I have lost 80 per cent of the benefit. But still at the back of my mind looms the thought of playing in the Southampton game. I missed the start of last season with my knee injury and wouldn't want to be ruled out again. We'll see what the next few days bring.

In the evening we go out for a meal with the Newells to celebrate Catherine's birthday at a local Italian restaurant. I keep well away from the seafood!

WEDNESDAY 17TH

Back in the full swing of things with the rest of the lads. A morning of crossing, shooting and finishing, before Tony Parkes asks me, Christ Sutton and Paul Warhurst to stay behind for some overtime – mainly sharpening up work, 30 metres sprinting, jogging and then sprinting again. I go home tired but feeling brilliant. I love every minute of it. For the first time I am more than hopeful of kicking off the new season.

THURSDAY 18TH

There is laughter all round when the club doc comes into the ground to tell me I'm free to step up my training now. He's staggered to learn I've been joining in with the rest of the squad and am in with a chance of facing Southampton. I tell the manager I want to play, though I accept the decision is entirely his. I know I daren't let the lads down by pretending to be fit when I'm not but I genuinely feel I have something to contribute.

FRIDAY 19TH

We leave early for Southampton. Me, Tim and the gaffer have arranged to meet the team bus at 11.00 a.m. at the M6 services, though predictably it's late. After a fairly trouble-free journey, we arrive and go out for half an hour's training at Eastleigh FC's ground. I am called upon to join in the set-piece work which is the biggest hint yet that I will be in the starting line-up. I sleep easily, knowing that I have a good chance of playing, perhaps just for an hour before I run out of legs.

SATURDAY 20TH

I share a room with Tim Flowers in the absence of Mike Newell and it's a totally new experience for me. I'm awakened by our goalkeeper's shouts from the bathroom at 7.00 a.m. He's reading the morning paper and yells out, 'I can't believe this, Kevin Keegan has left me out of his dream team.'

But he quickly endears himself to me by bringing me some cornflakes and a cup of tea. He could get the job permanently if he carries on like this. I nod off for a couple more hours before we all meet for a half-hour's stroll at 11.30. Lunch at midday – boiled chicken and baked beans for me, which is my usual pre-match meal, though I sometimes have poached egg on toast for a change. We have a team meeting at 12.45 and the team is announced, with Chris Sutton and myself both named in the starting line-up. The gaffer has a quick word about the opposition but doesn't dwell too much on them. I confirm that they will be using a sweeper, having spoken to my former Southampton team-mate Tommy Widdrington.

The Dell will always be a special place for me. It is where I was taught my trade as a footballer back in the days when it was by no means a glamorous way of life. I worked hard and played hard and learned all about discipline and obedience. All of the trainees had to carry out routine chores – like cleaning boots, sweeping out the dressing-room, disinfecting the medical room and any other odd jobs which needed doing.

The youth team coach, Dave Merrington, was my immediate boss and as a fellow Geordie I always got on with him. But it did not earn me any special privileges. Once when I was arguing that it was not my turn to do a particular job, Dave overheard and said, 'I'll show you whose turn it is, bonny lad. Be at the ground at seven o'clock in the morning, ready to start work.'

On another occasion, I left the tap running in the boot room and it flooded the medical room below. That made me very popular with my fellow apprentices because we were all made to run 50 laps around the pitch. Dave's argument was that it is a team game and we should share our punishment as well as our praise!

My reception at The Dell is fairly mixed with some jeers and some cheers. I except that. The kick-off approaches. It looked as if I wouldn't make it at one time but here I am, ready and excited about the start of a new campaign. A shiver runs down my spine.

What an anti-climax. Southampton score through Nicky Banger after a great ball from Matt Le Tissier. I have a great chance to equalise after I force a penalty when Francis Benali handles my shot which might just have crept into the net.

I commit the classic error of changing my mind. I decide to blast it but as I turn for my run-up, choose to place it. Don't ask me why. I put it too close to Bruce Grobbelaar who saves it comfortably. This is the second penalty miss of my career – both of them at The Dell. I don't think I'll take any more here.

But I make amends and manage to grab an equaliser. Chris Sutton nods the ball down to me and the Southampton players claim I handled the ball before scoring, but I don't believe I did. It's great to get off the mark, though we feel we did enough to get more out of the game than a 1-1 draw. The Press are all interested in talking about my partnership with Chris Sutton. I tell them it's early days yet but considering this is the first time we have played together, we've done OK and combined well for the goal.

I arrive home after the long trek back north at around 11.00 p.m., feeling absolutely shattered but satisfied with my day's work.

SUNDAY 21ST

I have to go in for treatment, having taken a kick on the hamstring. I then have a quiet afternoon in front of the box watching Leicester against Newcastle. I'm very impressed with Kevin Keegan's team, who win 3-1, though it's sad to see Peter Beardsley suffer another fractured cheekbone which will keep him out for a couple of months. Will they be able to sustain their challenge at the top without him?

MONDAY 22ND

I pick up my new car, a Mercedes 280, having traded in my two-year-old BMW for it. I suppose I'll get stick from the lads but Lainya will drive it mostly since I have a sponsored Rover for my own use. I don't train today because the hamstring is still a bit sore.

TUESDAY 23RD

More treatment in the morning and then Tim, Mike and I check into a local hotel in readiness for tonight's home game against Leicester. We arrive at the ground and no one is quite sure how to get to the dressing-rooms at the impressive new Ewood Park, but we manage to find our way with a little help. We soon find our way out on the field as well, especially Chris Sutton. He marks his home debut with his first goal for the club, heading in my cross, and then we combine to set up a chance for Henning Berg to score a second. I complete the scoring before the end to make it two goals in two games. Not bad for someone who was supposedly at death's door a week or so earlier. It could have been four of five if I had taken all my chances.

FRIDAY 26TH

A pleasant duty to perform today. There was a story in the local *Evening Telegraph* about a small boy who had his Rovers shirt stolen from him in the town. The club decide to give him a couple of replacements with No. 9 and Shearer on the back. I help to make the presentation and it's a delight to see the kid's face as he leaves with his new shirts and autographs. Then it's off to training for tomorrow's game against Coventry.

SATURDAY 27TH

We start very sloppily, though Steve Ogrizovic is in fine form in the Sky Blues goal. It remains at 0-0 until the final twenty minutes when the whole game is turned on its head by the sending off of Mick Quinn. He is penalised for handball, says something out of turn to the referee and gets his marching orders. We score from the free kick with a header from Chris Sutton who goes on to score a hat-trick in a 4-0 victory.

That takes a lot of pressure off Chris who has already taken a load of stick in the media because of his £5 million fee. That's the only way for a striker to silence criticism – score goals.

It has clearly been getting to Chris. He's not a particularly outgoing type but he's been exceptionally quiet and reserved since he arrived. This hat-trick is sure to bring him out of his shell a bit. He's already got a nickname – Trigger – after the character in *Only Fools and Horses*. But he's a great lad and a good partner to play alongside.

The Coventry game is the last but one for Phil Babb in their colours. I get the distinct impression that all the transfer speculation about a £3.6 million tag is starting to affect him. He certainly doesn't look the same player who performed so outstandingly in the World Cup, but I'm sure he'll soon rediscover his international form.

TUESDAY 30TH

After a morning training session we travel to London for the Arsenal game.

On the coach we hear the England squad announcement for the friendly against the United States of America. My name is among them and it still gives me a terrific buzz to learn I have been chosen for my country. It's something you never get complacent or blasé about. The big talking point is the inclusion of John Barnes because everyone assumed his England career was over. But he's still a class act. I've seen him on TV this season and he seems to have shed a lot of weight and worked very hard to get himself back into peak physical condition. Part of the problem with John stems from the wonder goal he scored early in his international career against Brazil when he beat a whole line of defenders before walking the ball into the net. It was always going to be difficult to top that but he's won 70-odd caps for England and you don't achieve that without being able to play.

When I arrive in London I arrange hotel rooms for the Wembley game for Mum and Dad and Jack Hixon, the scout who discovered me playing in the north-east when I was twelve.

Jack just turned up on the touchline one day when I was playing for the Newcastle City schoolboys team. His 'beat' is the whole of the north-east and any promising young players are sure to come under his gaze. He must have seen something he liked because he came along for a second look at me when I was in action for Wallsend Boys Club. Pretty soon afterwards Jack asked my dad if I would like to go and have a trial with Southampton. Dad's reply was 'Ask him yourself, he's old enough to make up his own mind.' That was typical of Dad. He wanted me to be responsible for my own actions and didn't want to put any pressure on me.

Of course, I was still a Newcastle United nut in those days and had been there for trials. A myth has developed since that Newcastle did not see me operate as a striker because I spent the whole of the trial playing in goal – but that was not really the case. I did take my turn between the posts, like everyone else at the session, but I had a fair crack of the whip playing out-field as well.

I jumped at the offer to go for trials at Southampton because I felt it would give me the chance to compare different clubs. Eventually I opted to sign for them on schoolboy forms, even if it meant turning my back on my beloved Newcastle. I had a feeling it would be a better career move because there would be more of an opportunity to break into the first team at an early age with the Saints. So it proved to be. Jack monitored my progress, just as he did with all the lads he took to The Dell, and over the years he has become part of the Shearer family.

He has been a major influence on my career and has cost me a fortune in telephone calls. Wherever I travel, at home or abroad, I give Jack a ring to chat about football and ask for his advice on a variety of matters. He scouts for Sunderland now with the same insight and love for the game he has always shown. Scouts like Jack are a breed apart. Many of them devote their lives to football – not for the financial rewards because they only pick up a few quid expenses and get their phone bills paid. When Jack recommended me to Southampton, he provided them with a player who was to become worth £3.3m but he did not do it for any personal financial reward. He did it for the pride of knowing he helped a football-crazy youngster take the first steps towards realising his ambitions.

I also remember to ring Michelle Rogers, the international secretary at the Football Association and ask her to book a car to pick up Tim Flowers and myself from Highbury after the game and take us to Burnham Beeches Hotel in Buckinghamshire, where the England squad will be gathering.

WEDNESDAY 31ST

We are put through an early morning training session in Regent's Park – not the most ideal location because there are so many people around and the surface is pretty awful.

Kenny Dalglish calls us together an hour and a half before the game to go through Arsenal's strengths and weaknesses. We know that they will be very strong defensively and can expect the match to be a tough physical one.

Tim Flowers pulls off a couple of good saves but we find ourselves right up against it when Jason Wilcox is sent off eight minutes after the interval for his second bookable offence. The second booking was for a silly tackle on Lee Dixon. Jason has been booked three times in five games already, but I think that's more to do with the new crackdown by referees than any extra agression on his part.

After being reduced to ten men, the gaffer sends Chris Sutton back to play alongside Colin Hendry and Tony Gale in a reinforced defence.

Someone remarks that for a £5 million striker, Chris looks a really good centre half. Tony Gale isn't a bad acquisition either for a free transfer. Ray Harford knew him from their days together at Fulham and he has come to Blackburn on a three-month contract. He also plays his part in a hard-earned goalless draw.

Tim and I travel to Burnham Beeches after the game and are the first of the England players to arrive. We kill some time while waiting for the others with a highly competitive game of snooker. The first to five frames has to pay for the table and I hand it to Tim on a plate by missing the final black over the pocket when I'm 4-3 down. The rest of the squad start to gather and Terry Venables calls us together for soup and sandwiches and a chat about next week's International.

SEPTEMBER 1994

FRIDAY 2ND

Training is taken up mostly with an eight-a-side game. Terry is a very straight-talking type of coach who gets on great with the lads. He concentrates on a lot of technical work with the ball but, surprising though it may seem, he doesn't differ too much from his predecessor Graham Taylor. Perhaps he emphasises the need to keep hold of the ball more, but that's not to say Graham was a long-ball merchant. He got stuck with that label at Watford but it was a bit unfair because he never advocated route one stuff with the England team. I owe a lot to Graham for helping to launch my international career and I admire him as a manager.

After training, the afternoon is taken up with some strenuous games of Sega golf. It's a hard life.

SATURDAY 3RD

Training is a repeat of the previous day with a small-sided game. We are given the rest of the day off so Tim and I decide to travel back to Blackburn. What a mistake. The traffic is so bad it takes us five hours to complete the journey. Still, it's worth it just to have a night's sleep in my own bed.

SUNDAY 4TH

I take Lainya and Chloe for Sunday lunch and leave to travel back to Burnham at 4.30 p.m. It's an even worse journey. It takes us almost six hours and we arrive at the England hotel 45 minutes late. We sneak in and no one notices.

MONDAY 5TH

Training consists of work on our team play and I start to get half an idea that the boss is going to play with two strikers up front. In my previous matches for Terry Venables I have been the lone striker waiting for support from midfield.

We are called together for an autograph-signing session in the afternoon when the squad have to put their signatures to around 500 footballs and England tops.

TUESDAY 6TH

The England team is announced to face the USA. I am named for my eleventh cap and it gives me the same thrill as when I won my first. The famous Terry Venables Christmas tree formation is abandoned in favour of a two-pronged strike force with Teddy Sheringham alongside myself. I never minded playing alone up front. It requires a lot of hard work and running but that's something I've always relished. Still, it'll be nice to have a bit of company because it can get a bit lonely up there all on your own.

The surprise choice is Barry Venison, who's been having a splendid season for Newcastle. The boss likes someone to operate just in front of the back four to break up the opposition's pattern of play – and Barry does this job well.

Tim Flowers seems a bit disappointed not to be given the nod ahead of David Seaman. My Blackburn mate has been in outstanding form in goal for us and was being tipped for the number one spot. He doesn't show his feelings outwardly at being overlooked, but is a bit quieter than usual.

WEDNESDAY 7TH

We work on set pieces at the morning training session and then snatch a few hours in bed. The butterflies start earlier than usual and we have tea and toast before leaving for Wembley at 5.45 p.m.

Before the kick-off there's a minute's silence for the former England captain Billy Wright who died at the weekend. I never met him but there isn't a person in the game who has a bad word to say about him. Tim, who started his career at Molineux, knew him and referred to him merely as Mr Wolves.

I get an early chance but hesitate because I think I am offside and scuff the shot ten or fifteen yards wide. Another similar opportunity comes my way soon afterwards and with the defence backing off me I put this one away inside the near post.

There's a bit of banter between myself and the bearded American defender Alexi Lalas over an article in the *News of the World* the previous weekend. I was quoted as saying I couldn't remember his name and his reply was that he would show me at Wembley. We have a laugh about it after he points out that he never said anything of the sort anyway.

My second goal comes ten minutes before half-time. Graeme Le Saux puts in a great cross and I get in front of Mr Lalas to score with a diving header. I couldn't have placed it any better and it flies into the bottom corner.

I have another headed chance before the interval but this time it's saved. I make contact with the back of Lalas' head and a big bump immediately comes up on the side of my face. Peter Beardsley's fractured cheekbone springs to mind. He has suffered the injury twice in successive seasons and I fear the worst. I am carried off but fortunately the half-time whistle is not too far away and I am able to have some ice-pack treatment on the knock. Soon I feel fine and start thinking of a hat-trick.

Unfortunately, no decent chances come my way in the second half and there is a general feeling of disappointment that we only score two goals. I cannot complain, though, because my record now reads five goals from eleven Internationals. There is already speculation that I could be on course to beat Bobby Charlton's England record of 49 goals. A bit premature, I would say, but I suppose time is on my side. I'm still only 24 (going on 34 according to some people).

I meet Mum and Dad and Jack Hixon and his wife after the game, have a quick drink and then head off home. I can't wait to see the family again and arrive home at 2.45 a.m.

THURSDAY 8TH

Any thoughts of a lie-in are shattered when Chloe wakes me at 7.00 a.m. to tell me about her visit to see Postman Pat in Liverpool while I was in London.

We have to report for training at 12 noon and I can't wait to get home to catch up with some sleep.

FRIDAY 9TH

There are a lot of nice things about me in the paper today, written as follow-ups to the England game. My friend Mr Lalas fills quite a few column inches by saying he thinks I would be a huge success in Italy. I don't know how he can make that judgement because he's only played one game for Padova so far and they lost that 5-0 to Sampdoria. It's all very flattering for me but it revives the speculation about me going to Italy all over again. I suppose it won't end until I eventually move there. All I can do is repeat the same responses about being happy at Blackburn and remind people once more that I still have almost two seasons left on my contract. And I still haven't started those Italian lessons!

SATURDAY 10TH

Everton are the visitors to Ewood Park today and they and their manager Mike Walker are already under the microscope after their disappointing start to the season.

I open the scoring with a 20-yarder after seventeen minutes and set up a second for Jason Wilcox just before half-time. On the hour we are awarded a penalty. It's my first spot-kick since I missed the one against Southampton on the opening day. This time I make my mind up where I'm going to place it and I stick to it. It's a lot harder to score from a penalty than people think. You can tuck them away in training without any problems but the pressure is on when you're out there in front of 26,000 people, with a goalkeeper of Neville Southall's ability and size in front of you. The fact that we are already 2-0 up helps my confidence and I slot it past Neville. He gets his own back in a way when he saves a diving header from me in the last five minutes in brilliant style. Another hat-trick opportunity slips by but if they keep coming in twos I won't complain.

Everton's new Nigerian signing Daniel Amokachi makes his debut but has little chance to shine because he's so well handled by our defence. There has been a lot of debate recently about the new influx of foreign players. It's quite normal for British clubs to scour the overseas market immediately after a World Cup and this year is no exception. There is an argument that too many imports can stifle the development of home-grown talent, but I believe if the quality of the signings is good enough it has to be right for the domestic game. There are some good bargains to be found on the Continent and even further afield, so it makes financial sense for clubs to cast their nets in that direction. Invariably the newcomers create big interest at the turnstiles, so that's another sound reason for the recruitment of overseas players. I have been particularly impressed by Jurgen Klinsmann, Tottenham's German recruit. He came here with a reputation among English fans as a striker whose main claim to fame was his ability to con referees. He has soon got rid of that and won a lot of doubters over with his hard work and goal-scoring ability. He's a great example of why the foreign legion is good for the game here.

TUESDAY 13TH

The day starts off badly and gets worse. On midweek matchdays, Tim Flowers, Mike Newell and I like to book into a Blackburn hotel for the afternoon to avoid making the journey home after training. We are making our big entry into the European competition against Trelleborg from Sweden in the UEFA Cup tonight, so we ring up our regular place, the Dunkenhalgh Hotel, which is fully booked. We manage to find an alternative but is this break in our regular routine an unlucky omen?

Everyone is asking how many goals we'll put past the Swedish part-timers, which is a dangerous way of thinking. So it proves to be. We are terrible. Every player from position one to eleven seems to have an off-day and that doesn't happen very often. To be fair to Trelleborg, they defend very well and raise their game to make life very difficult for us before pinching a goal to win 1-0. The dressing-room is a depressing place afterwards but there are no angry words or impromptu inquests. The best time to examine what went wrong is when the dust has settled. Our only consolation is that we have another bite at the cherry in the second leg. We all know we are capable of scoring goals against them and that lifts our spirits a bit.

THURSDAY 15TH

There's a team meeting to discuss the Trelleborg defeat. All we can do is hold our hands up and admit that we didn't play well. It is agreed that we haven't become a bad team overnight and that it was just a one-off mishap which can be put right in the return game. We have a hard training session to burn off our frustration.

Back home our new kitchen is 90 per cent complete and we have actually begun cooking in it again. The profits at the local restaurant around the corner from us are about to suffer because it's been our regular eating place for so long.

FRIDAY 16TH

I go into the ground early today because our coach driver Paul Stone wants a picture taken with me for his office. I am happy to oblige.

After training I give Tim a lift to pick up his new Land Rover Discovery but it proves to be a wasted journey because the insurance cover note has not turned up.

Lainya's dad Steve has been with us this week helping to put the finishing touches to the kitchen. Her mum Jenny and brother Gareth are joining us for the weekend and I drive over to Liverpool airport to pick them up.

SATURDAY 17TH

Training as usual today because our game this weekend is the live Sky game against Chelsea on Sunday. We are now installed in our new headquarters at Brockhall, a magnificent new facility which must have cost Jack Walker another tidy sum. The dressing-rooms are still being built and once they are finished, complete with sauna and jacuzzi, the whole complex will be among the best in the Premiership. Another indication that no expense is being spared to put Rovers on top of the pile.

We travel down to London after training and brace ourselves for the traffic nightmares of the M6, but it isn't too bad this time and the journey to the Hilton Hotel in Cobham only takes about four hours. Hats off to our coach driver Paul for once, because he usually manages to find all available jams. We keep up to date with the football news by listening to Radio Five on the way down and, after dinner, stay up for *Match of the Day* on TV.

SUNDAY 18TH

We take an early lead with a six-yard box scramble after a great cross by Graeme Le Saux. Eventually it is put down to an own goal by Erland Johnsen and although I'm close to the action I can't really claim it. Maybe if the TV cameras hadn't been there, I might have tried to nick it. John Spencer equalises just after half-time but Chris Sutton chalks up another goal to give us the three points. I'm having second thoughts about Chris – he's not the quiet lad I first thought he was. He has become one of the lads now and isn't afraid to let his feelings be known.

I've taken a couple of knocks on my ankle and back which require ice treatment, but we are soon heading back to the hotel after the game because we are staying overnight. We are halfway back to the Hilton when we suddenly realise our physio Mike Pettigrew isn't on board. Everyone was told to be ready to leave Stamford Bridge at 7.00 p.m. but for some reason we depart a minute early and Mike is left behind. Any thoughts of going back for him are soon dismissed. A car is arranged to collect him and I'm quite relieved to see Mike because I need some further treatment on my injuries.

MONDAY 19TH

We depart for home at around 12.30 p.m. and are making good progress until the coach suddenly grinds to a halt on the M42 after a couple of hours. Would you believe it? We've run out of fuel. Paul the driver insists he put 100 gallons in two days before but is having trouble with his fuel gauge. You can imagine the stick he receives from the lads. We are on the move again after an hour's delay and arrive home at 6.30 p.m.

TUESDAY 20TH

I'm in for treatment on my injuries and I'm hopeful of being in the team for tonight's Coca-Cola Cup tie against Birmingham because I've played with a lot worse. I'm a bit surprised therefore, when the boss announces the team at around 6.30 p.m. and says he is giving me a rest to allow the knocks to recover properly. Jason Wilcox and Chris Sutton score the goals in a comfortable victory for us. That's Chris's sixth in seven games and all those chants of 'What a waste of money' are starting to look a bit foolish. I sit and watch in the stands, twiddling my thumbs, tapping my feet and wishing I was out there playing. I'm one of the world's worst spectators.

WEDNESDAY 21ST

It's Chloe's second birthday so we're up early opening her presents. The biggest thrill she has is ripping the wrapping paper apart and creating a huge mess but she loves the new bike we've bought her.

After treatment at the ground, I'm back home in the afternoon for Chloe's party, attended by some of her friends and Lainya's sister Shona and her fiancé Paul.

The main football news today is the announcement of Gary Lineker's retirement from the game at the end of his season in Japan in November. I had the privilege of playing alongside Gary for England and fully appreciate what a tremendous goalscorer he was. He was the sort of player who came alive in the penalty box and thrived on half-chances.

He scored 48 goals for England – just one behind Bobby Charlton's all-time record. If I can score half that many international goals I'll be pleased, though as a goal-hungry striker not completely satisfied.

The other thing I admire Gary for is how well he handles the media. He is always friendly, helpful and approachable and finds the right thing to say at the right time. I'm sure that helped create his wholesome image and was why he was so rarely criticised in the Press.

THURSDAY 22ND

Mike Newell and I travel in for treatment while the rest of the players have a day off. We can't stand the thought of Tim Flowers having a lie-in, so we ring him at 9.15. He swears he's up and about, so we call him again fifteen minutes later to make sure he hasn't gone back to sleep.

Tim has been one of my best mates from the day he joined Southampton from Wolves as a youngster. Even then he had all the makings of a great goalkeeper and I remember saying to my dad a couple of months after he arrived, 'Tim will play for England one day.' He is a fanatical trainer and at The Dell, he had two brilliant teachers in Peter Shilton and John Burridge who taught him a lot about dedication as well as technique. Tim loves a laugh and a joke but when it's time for work he puts himself through a punishing routine.

When it became obvious that Southampton were willing to sell him, I recall saying to Kenny Dalglish, 'If you are considering looking for a new goalkeeper Tim's your man. He's not only a great keeper, but a good lad and a thorough professional who hates taking a day off.' I used to ring Tim, urging him to sign for us if he got the chance and I know Neil Ruddock was on at him all the time to join Liverpool. Eventually he made the right choice and I reckon he has become the top goalkeeper in the country. His work rate is even more phenomenal now and he considers it an insult if anyone beats him with a shot – even in training.

FRIDAY 23RD

Tim drives us to the ground in his new Land Rover Discovery. He's like a kid with a new toy. 'Don't touch that . . . don't break that', which naturally encourages Mike and myself to tamper with all the gadgets in sight. Tim is working apart from the other lads with the goalkeeping coach Terry Gennoe today, so someone moves his vehicle to another parking spot while he is away. 'Who's been in my Discovery?' he asks when he returns. We tell him we took it screaming down the motorway to run it in for him. He's furious and never says a word to Mike or myself on the way home. I've never known him this quiet, even when he was overlooked for the last England game. I think we may have upset him . . .

SATURDAY 24TH

Tim travels into the ground on his own on matchdays so we don't know whether he's still upset. Eventually Mike and I put him out of his misery and tell him we were only joking and no one had taken his Discovery for a joyride.

Villa are the visitors today and it promises to be an entertaining game against a team who like to attack. So it proves to be. I score from a penalty which makes it two out of three so far this season. I'm particularly chuffed about this one because the Villa keeper Mark Bosnich has a reputation for saving penalties. Again I make my mind up about where I'm going to place it and stick to my guns. Chris Sutton adds a second and already we can envisage the headlines about the multi-million strike force grabbing all the glory. I score a third when Tim Flowers acts as playmaker with a big clearance which Chris Sutton heads on to leave me with a simple chance to convert. This is easily our best display of the season and it is only spoiled by a late Villa goal from Ugo Ehiogu which is the first we have conceded at home in the League. Naturally the media want to talk about my partnership with Chris again. We are getting to learn about each other's game and our combined scoring record is good, but there is still more to come. Our overall fitness and sharpness is still not

100 per cent because of the amount of pre-season training we missed but we are getting there. Tonight's League table shows Blackburn second behind Newcastle – a nice feeling but no one takes too much notice of it at this stage of the season. There's a long, hard campaign ahead of us.

SUNDAY 25TH

We train today because of the journey to Sweden for the second leg of the UEFA Cup tomorrow. It's just a loosener and then back home for a typical Sunday with the family.

MONDAY 26TH

We meet up at Blackpool airport for the flight to Malmo and, wonder of wonders, the plane takes off on time for Blackburn's first excursion on to foreign soil for a competitive match. After checking into our hotel, we depart almost straight away for a five o'clock training session. Tony Parkes has forgotten to pack my Umbro training boots so I have to borrow Tim Sherwood's. They're one size too big but I'll get by with them without any problems – or so I think.

TUESDAY 27TH

A photographer snapped me in training yesterday and a picture of me appears in the *Daily Mail* today, wearing Asics boots. Umbro representatives are straight on the phone to my business manager Tony Stephens back in England but his explanation manages to placate them. Fortunately, my Umbro match boots have been packed and I can wear them for the game – which is just as well. Umbro Brazil have telephoned the UK to say that the photograph had appeared out there! The world gets smaller.

In training this morning, I do some finishing work – or at least I try to. Tim Flowers is unbeatable in goal. He stops everything we can fire at him from any range. That's a good sign for tonight's match against Trelleborg. The boss's team talk emphasises that we have a second chance to put things right after the disastrous first leg and we dare not waste it. We are in a confident mood after Saturday's win over Villa but still know we can't afford to take anything for granted against the Swedish part-timers.

We get off to a dream start when Chris Sutton volleys us into the lead after sixteen minutes but they equalise early in the second half to go back in front on aggregate. It looks as if we'll go through on the away goals rule when I score with about seven minutes to go, but Joachim Karlsson stuns us a couple of minutes later with a second equaliser. We all think he's offside but it's no good complaining. We shouldn't have allowed him that much space.

We go out on a 3-2 aggregate score at the first hurdle and inevitably the inquests begin among the media experts. The popular view is that we have a style of play which is not suited to Europe. While that is an unfair accusation, it is true that in both games we have not done ourselves justice. When we were chasing the game at the end of both legs we tended to run out of ideas and lump the ball forward to the strikers and hope for the best. If you do that, you risk giving the ball away and even against a team of part-timers it is very difficult to win it back when the opposition have no need to commit themselves to attack. I think this is where we have missed the injured David Batty. As well as being a great little competitor, he provides us with variety because he can pass it long and short. The ideal way of playing, whatever the opposition, is to mix and match your styles and I am afraid in the UEFA Cup we failed to do that well enough.

This is the biggest disappointment of my career – bigger even than the defeat suffered by England in Holland, which more or less wrecked our World Cup qualifying hopes. Then I had just forced my way back into the England reckoning and was just pleased to be involved on the international scene again. Here in Sweden we have let ourselves, Jack Walker and the fans down by going out at the first hurdle. We worked so hard to qualify for Europe by finishing in the runners-up spot last season and we've blown it at the first attempt. When we arrive at Malmo airport for the journey home we are greeted by the cheers of the 600 or so Blackburn fans who have made the expensive trip to support us. No one can blame them if they give us a hard time, but they tell us to hold our heads up and assure us they are still behind us. That's nice but it's still a very quiet flight home and we troop home to bed at 3.45 a.m. – tired and dejected.

WEDNESDAY 28TH

I am woken at 7.45 by Chloe, yelling out, 'Daddy, monkeys.' I promised to take my daughter to Knowsley Safari Park and the result of last night is not going to spoil her fun. We spend most of the day there with friends Debbie and Lee from Southampton and it helps take my mind off the defeat. We get a Chinese take-away on the way home and sit watching Manchester United's goalless draw against Galatasaray in the European Cup. I just about manage to stay awake.

THURSDAY 29TH

A hard training session to try to rid ourselves of the misery of Sweden and focus on Saturday's trip to Norwich. Lainya has gone home to Southampton for a few days so I visit the Newells for tea and stay to watch the Aston Villa-Inter Milan game. It's a real thriller with Villa going through on penalties. Naturally, I start to think of what might have been and whether, if we had played a bigger name club, we would have been more fired up for it. Seeing Villa go through in such style and glory makes our departure from Europe even harder to swallow.

FRIDAY 30TH

After a four-and-a-half hour coach trip to Norwich, we train and get back to our hotel to check the UEFA Cup draw on Teletext. There are big groans from Tim and myself when we see that Trelleborg are playing Lazio. What a game that could have been for us.

OCTOBER 1994

SATURDAY 1ST

I ring David Platt in Italy, after learning that he's suffered a knee injury midweek. It appears to be cartilage damage and he expects to be out of action for three to four weeks which will mean him missing the next England game against Romania. I know what he's going through but he seems reasonably cheerful.

The Norwich game goes according to the script when Chris Sutton puts us ahead against his old club and we are knocking the ball around well. It seems as if the Trelleborg defeat has been banished from our minds. Then our luck changes. Norwich score a lucky equaliser when Mark Bowen's shot is deflected past Tim Flowers and John Newsome gets an even flukier winner in the second half, the ball skidding off his non-striking foot and looping into the net. Another silent journey home at the end of a week we would rather forget.

SUNDAY 2ND

It never rains but it pours. I take the dog for a walk, the heavens open and I get drenched. Lainya is still away in Southampton, so I invite myself to neighbour Neil Ruddock's home for lunch. I'll eat anywhere there is a spare plate and the Liverpool defender and his wife Sarah make me very welcome. Neil has been round to our house while I was away in Norwich to feed the dog. He leaves some messages lying around like, 'Would you like Swedes for Sunday lunch?' I get my own back by pinning an up-to-date League table on his door which shows Blackburn in second place and Liverpool fifth.

But we are pushed down to third place this afternoon by Nottingham Forest's 3-2 win over QPR with Stan Collymore hitting the late winner.

Stan is one of a growing group of strikers who are hitting the headlines and a load of goals. Newcastle's Andy Cole and our own Chris Sutton are also being mentioned as England candidates. I'll have to keep on my toes with this lot around.

MONDAY 3RD

I go to Tim Flowers' for tea after training and then we meet the coach on the M6 to travel to Birmingham for tomorrow's Coca-Cola Cup second leg. There's an England squad announcement today for the match against Romania on Wednesday week. The big news is that Andy Cole has been overlooked which stirs up a lot of media reaction. It appears that he's got a problem with shin splints, which is the reason Kevin Keegan gives for his absence. Terry Venables sticks to myself, Teddy Sheringham, Les Ferdinand and Ian Wright for his strike force, so the young pretenders have to wait a little longer. Newcastle's Robert Lee is included and is being tipped to replace David Platt in midfield.

TUESDAY 4TH

Training is optional because it's matchday. I decide, as usual, to join in a five-a-side. Nothing too strenuous – just enough to get a sweat on. Back at the hotel, I ask the coach driver Paul to get me a copy of the new book *Princess in Love*, which has attracted a massive amount of coverage in the newspapers. I am quite interested in the royal family – especially where the Princess of Wales is concerned!

We make a good start against Birmingham and only a tremendous save by their keeper Ian Bennett stops me from extending our aggregate lead early in the game. The Second Division club score after fifteen minutes and suddenly the heat is on us. The atmosphere their crowd generate is electric and we really have to dig deep to keep our advantage but once Chris Sutton equalises in the second half, it's game over. After a quiet drink in the players' lounge, we board the coach to leave at 10.30 p.m. – or so we think.

All the electrics have packed up and Paul reckons it should be sorted in about half an hour. When the bus is still immobile 30 minutes later, a few of us get off and try to give it a bump start but that doesn't work. We are sitting around in complete darkness and you can imagine the stick poor old Paul is getting about the new coach which cost £195,000. At 11.30 there is still no sign of life. Midnight – still nothing. By 12.30 some of us have had enough, so we call for three taxis to take us home. The journey costs £75 per car but it's better than hanging around in the dark. Ironically the bus sparks into life fifteen minutes after we speed away from the scene. We get home at around 2.45, when we had expected to be back just before midnight. Lainya has arrived back home from Southampton with her mum and dad but I warned her in advance not to wait up.

THURSDAY 6TH

Back in training after being given yesterday off, but first I do an interview with Richard Bott of the *Sunday Express* about the strikers I have partnered playing for England. Home for a rest and I certainly feel like one after playing three games in seven days. A footballer's routine settles into a very fixed pattern at this stage of the season. Train-rest-play-rest-train and so on. The amount of fixtures, domestic and international, leaves little time for anything else. Not that I'm complaining. It's been like this ever since I started as a professional and it's a lifestyle I wouldn't change for anything. There is an argument that we play so much competitive football that it allows no time for players to work on their individual skills, but I don't go along with that view. I have always stayed behind after training if I felt the need to work on a part of my game which was not up to standard and will continue to do so. I think I speak for the majority of players when I say I would rather play games than train. The only problem with a pile-up of fixtures is that, if you pick up an injury, it's so much harder to get rid of it when one match follows so rapidly after another.

SATURDAY 8TH

I pack an extra bag because a group of us are travelling down to link up with the England squad straight after tomorrow's game against Newcastle. After a training session at Ewood Park, we travel up to the north-east, my home territory. I grew up as a Newcastle fanatic, so this is an emotional game for me against the top-of-the-table team managed by the man I idolised as a kid – Kevin Keegan. Kenny Dalglish joins me before dinner to make a cheque presentation of £500 donated by Milligans, a local bakery firm, to Cramlington Juniors for whom I played as a lad. After the meal I have an enjoyable hour with my parents, sister Karen and her husband Wayne. I go back to my room at 9.15 p.m. and Tim takes the mickey out of me as I bury my head in *Princess in Love*. We watch Liverpool v Aston Villa on *Match of the Day* and have a right good laugh at Neil Ruddock and his celebration jig after scoring a goal in the 3-2 win. We think about ringing him but decide there is no way he'll be in on a Saturday night.

SUNDAY 9TH

We call Neil Ruddock and his explanation is that he doesn't score that many goals and didn't quite know what to do. A likely story. Tim is out early, travelling with the coach driver to the ground to start his preparations and help lay the kit out. He forgets my cornflakes. Much more of that and I'll have to get another unpaid servant . . .

There's a lot of coverage in the Sunday papers about the game – much of it focusing on the supposed showdown between Andy Cole and myself. I get a lot of ribbing about a so-called 'pin-up' picture in the *Sunday People* magazine, which shows me in just a pair of shorts. I remember the shot. It was taken at the European Championships three years ago when I was young, naïve and willing to pose for anything. Everyone – family, teammates, management – give me a terrible time about it. They reckon I have put on about a stone since it was taken. Very embarrassing.

There's a marvellous atmosphere at St James's Park and we start the game exceptionally well. We are rewarded when we get a penalty for a foul on Jason Wilcox. I'm a bit nervous because this one is in front of the Gallowgate End where I used to stand and support Newcastle, but I get an extra buzz when I convert it. We stay on top and are unfortunate several times not to score the goal which would have put the match out of their reach. Newcastle launch a big assault at the finish but it looks like we have weathered it when Tim makes a brilliant stop with a few minutes left. But again the run of the ball is against us. Steve Howey's effort is cleared off the line by Jason Wilcox, it hits Tim on the back and goes into the net. Another unlucky deflection, another goal and we are feeling very disappointed after playing so well but having to share the points.

I spend an hour in the players' lounge after the game with my friends and family but have to leave for Newcastle airport where a group of us fly by private jet to London to link up with the England squad for Wednesday's game against Romania at Wembley. Our party includes Kevin Keegan, who's in charge of the Under 21 squad playing Austria in Vienna on Tuesday. It's only a 50-minute flight but it's a pleasure to be able to spend some time in the company of my boyhood hero.

I was not alone in worshipping Keegan. When he signed for Newcastle as a player he was like the pied piper. Thousands upon thousands of kids flocked to the club to watch him train and play and drooled over his skills and incredible enthusiasm. I won a competition in a local newspaper to spend a day at the training ground with Kevin and the rest of the team and I was walking on air for several days. I also stood on the Gallowgate End shouting my head off when he made his debut against Queen's Park Rangers. The moment he scored with a diving header at our end will live with me forever. I studied and copied loads of players but Keegan was my number one. He made as much impact on the club as a player back then as he has done as a manager and he will live in Newcastle United folklore as long as there is a football club.

Even Kevin will admit, though, that his team were fortunate to get a draw today. At the England team hotel, there is a repeat of the Sky TV coverage of the game and it confirms my view that we were extremely unlucky not to win.

MONDAY 10TH

Training starts at Bisham Abbey at 10 a.m. but I'm a late starter. I need a visit to the hospital for a check on my little finger which was dislocated in yesterday's game. There is no serious damage. I soon get into the swing of things and join in the small-sided game.

TUESDAY 11TH

Terry Venables reads out the team and there are no real surprises because everyone had forecast that Matthew Le Tissier would replace the injured Peter Beardsley and Robert Lee would get his first start in place of David Platt. I know what Matt is capable of having seen and admired him at close quarters when we were team-mates at Southampton. He's immensely skilful but one of the most laidback people you could wish to meet – on and off the field. You can never rush him into anything.

WEDNESDAY 12TH

Set-piece work for attack and defence takes up most of the training time and, after an afternoon's rest, we leave for Wembley at 5.45 p.m. I have arranged tickets for Lainya's dad and brother who have come up from Southampton for the game. We don't start particularly well and it is no surprise when Illie Dumitrescu gives Romania the lead. Robert Lee equalises just before half-time, latching on to my header and tucking it away well. It's a goal on his full debut and a moment he will never forget. We have one or two half-chances in the second half, including a shot from me which hits a defender on the line. It isn't a great performance by us but a draw is not a bad achievement against one of the best sides to emerge from the World Cup. I meet Lainya's dad and brother in the players' lounge and after a chat I leave to make the journey home. Outside, Brian Woolnough of the *Sun* collars me and says Gheorghe Popescu had claimed I deliberately elbowed one of his Romanian team-mates. I reply that he is entitled to his opinion but don't really want to get drawn into a big row. The truth is one of their players grabbed me by the shirt and dragged me back. I just brushed him off me, though not with any really forceful contact. I wonder whether the Press will make an issue out of it. Paul drives us home and we arrive back at 3 a.m.

THURSDAY 13TH

We are in for training at 1 p.m., though it is basically to see whether the international players – Tim Flowers, Graeme Le Saux, myself, Colin Hendry and Henning Berg – have come through our games without mishap.

I have left my car at Tim's house and after picking it up, a female police officer pulls me over and books me for doing 42 mph in a 30 mph limit. It costs me a £40 fixed penalty fine and three points on my licence – my first ever. That'll teach me to be more careful.

FRIDAY 14TH

Tim Flowers manages to liven up the atmosphere before training today – at my expense. He has found a cutting from the Portsmouth paper, the *News*, which shows me in cartoon form and refers to me as Mr Mogadon and the Nigel Mansell of football. Apparently, this is a reference to my boring interview style on television. Very amusing. Of course, Tim does not show many people. He just pins it up in the dressing-room for everyone to see.

My goalkeeping pal also reckons he has heard that Nigel Mansell is suing for libel over this article because he is so annoyed at being compared with anyone as unexciting as me. Tim really believes he is funny. It raises an interesting thought, though. Players are often placed in potentially awkward situations after live games when we are thrust in front of the cameras with a microphone shoved under our noses. We have had no training for this type of thing and we have to learn quickly how to think on our feet when faced with tricky questions. I used to be nervous about the prospect of being interviewed. Fortunately I have never embarrassed myself on camera and handle TV appearances quite comfortably now even if, according to Mr Flowers, I put half the country to sleep.

Mum and Dad travel down for tomorrow's game against Liverpool and we have a quiet night at home.

SATURDAY 15TH

I have a lie-in until eleven and have my pre-match meal at home before travelling to the ground. We fall behind to yet another deflected goal. Robbie Fowler's shot hits Tony Gale and although Tim gets a hand to it he can't prevent it from going in. Mark Atkins equalises and I pull the ball back for Chris Sutton to give us a 2-1 lead. John Barnes puts the scores level but Chris settles it with a late winner for us. My mate Neil Ruddock is up against me today and there's some friendly banter between us. When he tackles me, he tells me to get up and stop cheating.

Ruddock is another one of the ex-Southampton brigade who have remained close friends after moving on to bigger clubs. He signed for the Saints from Millwall and claims I was responsible for clinching his transfer. He had played against me in a reserve game for Millwall and insists he marked me out of the game so effectively that Southampton could not wait to sign him. That may be a slight exaggeration but I admit he is a defender I would rather have on my side. He left Southampton for Tottenham before I joined Blackburn and, when he became unsettled at White Hart Lane, I did my best to try to persuade him to join Rovers. He chose Liverpool instead but we still ended up living in the same road. He is larger than life and a very loud character but he is great company and our two families socialise a lot. He and his wife Sarah are also very good dog-sitters and take care of Candy whenever we are away from home.

There's an interesting incident in the first half when I am running clean through towards the Liverpool goal. Chris Sutton is coming back in the opposite direction – in an offside position but not interfering with play. Under the new directive to referees, no offside should be given but the linesman's flag goes up. I have a few words to say to the referee Brian Hill and he tells me to leave it for now but to see him in the players' tunnel at half-time. He admits that a mistake was made. Honest of him, but it's little consolation to me because it cost me a good chance of scoring a goal.

After the game Neil and I join our wives for a drink in the players' lounge. Chloe has started coming to the games and loves shouting and clapping at every opportunity.

MONDAY 17TH

A day off and we take Chloe for lunch at McDonalds before visiting the hospital for Lainya's check-up at two o'clock. She is 34 weeks pregnant now and this is the last scan before the birth. Everything is in order. The nurse is careful not to give any secrets away about whether it's a boy or a girl. At first, she refers to it as a 'she' then a 'he'. Chloe has already made her mind up about the baby's sex. She refers to it as Baby Bob. I haven't a clue why.

It's my turn to visit the hospital in the evening. When I had the clash of heads with the American defender Lalas in the international game at Wembley, a bump came up on the side of my head and it's slowly been getting bigger. It has caused an artery to split and there's a danger it will burst open if I get another knock on it. I have it removed under local anaesthetic and am in and out of hospital within an hour. It's painless, though I do wake up in the middle of the night with a bit of a headache. I take a couple of painkillers and soon go back to sleep.

TUESDAY 18TH

No midweek game because we are out of Europe, so there's not a ball in sight in training. A hard running session with 40 minutes of half and three-quarter pace jogging. Graeme Le Saux and Jason Wilcox are the front runners. I occupy my usual place near the back.

I'm getting a bit worried because my current car insurance certificate hasn't arrived in the post and I need to present it at the police station by midnight on Thursday. I ring up the company and they insist it's in the post.

WEDNESDAY 19TH

Another day off and I get my new car phone fitted. In the afternoon I ring Mike Newell to wish him all the best on his comeback game for the reserves against Nottingham Forest. My insurance documents arrive in the second post and I take them to the police station. The officer on duty there tells me I was treated a bit harshly by the policewoman, who could have let me off with a warning. He insists I should consider myself lucky though. I could be married to her.

In the evening I settle down to watch Manchester United's European Cup game against Barcelona. It's a terrific match with United playing at 100 mph and Barcelona using a slower, more patient build-up. The fascinating contrast of styles ends in a 2-2 draw. Lee Sharpe is the outstanding player on the field and crowns his performance with a marvellous back-heel flick for United's second goal.

Mike Newell rings me later on his way back from the reserve game at Forest. We have won 2-1 and he has scored on his return, so it looks like there'll be more competition for first team places soon. Mike and I hit it off straightaway when I first signed for Rovers. I decided fairly soon that I wanted to live in the Merseyside area and initially we rented a house in Southport not far from Mike. We got to know each other on the golf course when we enjoyed quite a few rounds with Kenny Dalglish. Our budding friendship helped me on the field because I had just completed my record-breaking move and any assistance I could get was gratefully received. I could have asked for no better partner than Mike Newell, a strong character and powerful striker, who is brave and unselfish. He made it easy for me to settle into the team. It was important for me to make a good start with the big price tag around my neck and Mike helped create a lot of goals for me with his skills and strength. He has not enjoyed the best of fortune this season because strained knee ligaments have kept him on the sidelines but, even while he is injured, he is a great lad to have around the dressing room.

THURSDAY 20TH

A session in the weights room before training today. Afterwards I spend half an hour with Julie, one of our helpful office staff, sorting out some of the mail which has stacked up while she has been away on maternity leave. It's mostly pictures and other items which have been sent in to be autographed.

Some letters are slightly more unusual. I have had a couple from girls enclosing pictures of themselves in various stages of undress and asking me to meet them. I don't think it would be quite right for a family man to accept their invitations and Lainya and I just have a good laugh about them. Other items in the post which are unsigned and insulting go straight into the bin but I try to answer as many as possible, especially if young kids and charities have sent them.

FRIDAY 21ST

I've been asked to help out with a video for the Professional Footballers' Association as part of their campaign against drug and alcohol abuse. I record my piece this morning. It's going to be sent to all clubs and played to young trainees, warning them of the dangers involved. I have never been aware of any problem as far as drink or drugs are concerned in the game, but I suppose it is part of the hazards of growing up today and it has to be stamped out before it creeps into our profession. It's the last thing we want in our game.

SATURDAY 22ND

Another training day because we play Manchester United tomorrow in the live TV game. My eight-a-side team is beaten again – our third defeat on the trot. It includes the senior management staff, myself, Colin Hendry, Mike Newell, Bobby Mimms and Henning Berg. How can we possibly get beaten with so much quality involved?

These training matches can become very competitive with the rivalry between the respective teams pretty serious. They can be spiced up even more with the occasional bet. Last season I was involved in an ongoing challenge with Kevin Moran. We would pay each other £10 for scoring two or more goals in any game and I finished the season £80 in debt to him. I didn't pay him immediately and asked him if he fancied double or quits if I scored against him in a testimonial match between a Premiership XI and a Republic of Ireland team at Lansdowne Road. I managed to grab a goal in the second half which wiped my slate clean.

SUNDAY 23RD

Lainya's dad and brother have been staying with us this week, finishing off the roof in the utility room, and they have stayed on to watch the United game.

We make a great start in front of a full house at Ewood Park. We are well on top and fully deserve the lead given to us by Paul Warhurst's long range shot. Then disaster strikes when the referee Gerald Ashby gives a penalty for a challenge by Henning Berg on Lee Sharpe and shows our defender the red card. I am 70 yards further away from the incident than the ref and I can see that it's not a penalty. I would imagine just about everyone else in the ground – even the most die-hard United fans – think exactly the same. It wouldn't be so bad if Mr Ashby had just awarded the spot-kick, but to have to play the rest of the game with just ten men against a team of United's quality is too much to ask. It kills the game for us. Eric Cantona converts the penalty and, though Colin Hendry puts us back in front in the second half, we are always up against it. A goal from Mark Hughes and two from Andrei Kanchelskis give United a 4-2 victory. If there is any consolation for us it's that when both teams were at full strength, we were far and away the better side. In fact, in virtually all of our games against United over the last couple of seasons we have looked better than them. Of course, they can point to two successful Championship campaigns and I accept that this is a fairly powerful counter-argument. If today's game does anything it destroys the notion that United are only interested in winning the European Cup this season. They are not going to give up the title without one hell of a scrap and you have to admire their professionalism.

When I get home I watch a video of the game and it confirms everything I felt at the time. We were unfortunate. To make matters worse our unbeaten home record which stretches back thirteen months is shattered.

MONDAY 24TH

The same talking points are still being debated today – the penalty and the sending off. It seems we may be appealing against Henning's sending off and while that might mean he escapes a ban it won't alter the outcome of the game.

We have to get our minds off the United game now, though, and focus on Wednesday's Coca-Cola Cup tie against Coventry.

Training is fairly light-hearted to lift everyone's spirits. Tony Parkes and Chris Sutton are the jokers in the pack. In between the laughs, we enjoy a game of head tennis in the gym.

WEDNESDAY 26TH

I travel in with Tim and Mike and we have a good soak in the bath before heading off for an afternoon nap at the hotel. This is an important game for us because we cannot allow Sunday's defeat to weigh too heavily on our minds and wreck the rest of the season. It is difficult to get motivated, though. We've played in front of 35,000 at Newcastle, 31,000 against Liverpool and another 31,000 against United. For the Coventry game the attendance is down to 13,000. I'm not sure where all the missing fans have gone, but I suppose finance has something to do with it. It isn't cheap to watch football these days and understandably fans will save their money to watch games against more glamorous opponents.

It's hard to lift ourselves and it takes us fifteen to twenty minutes to get into our stride. I manage to grab a couple of goals to give us a 2-0 victory and that puts me level with Chris Sutton on twelve goals – ten for Blackburn and two for England.

There's not really a great rivalry between us to see who scores the most goals, but it's good that both of us are up among the League's leading scorers. Some sections of the Press have started referring to us as the SAS (Sutton and Shearer), but thankfully the other lads haven't latched on to it yet. When they do we'll get slaughtered.

FRIDAY 28TH

Lainya's dad and brother are due to go home today but they had a bit of a mishap with their fishing nets down on the beach near our house. They laid them out a couple of days ago but forgot to check the tides and are now having to stay on until Monday to retrieve them when the tide goes out. There won't be any fish in them – just debris washed ashore by the sea.

We travel to Nottingham for tomorrow's match against Forest after a normal training session. Lainya's nan and grandad, Joyce and Ray, have travelled up from Southampton to keep her company while I'm away.

SATURDAY 29TH

In the team meeting before the game, the gaffer explains he is leaving out Tony Gale and switching Paul Warhurst into the back four to cope with Bryan Roy's pace. The Dutch striker has been running amok this season and is clearly going to be their dangerman, especially as his partner Stan Collymore is ruled out with a hamstring strain.

We go a goal up in the first half through Chris Sutton and he takes his total for the season to fourteen with another after the interval. It's not a vintage attacking display from us but we all graft like hell for our 2-0 victory. After the misfortune we've been suffering recently, I think there's a concerted effort by the lads to grind out the points and try to ensure we are not prone to any more unnecessary lapses.

It's a much happier journey home than we have been used to of late. Mike, Tim and myself and our respective wives round off a good day with a very pleasant night out at our local Chinese restaurant. It's a joint birthday celebration for Tim's wife Jane and for Lainya, who's 24 on Tuesday.

MONDAY 31ST

I took a pile of signed photographs into the club offices today to distribute to the hundreds of people who write in for autographs. My boot sponsors, Umbro, provide the pictures and I find if I sign a batch of them in one go and leave them at the club, it speeds up the whole process. I'm grateful to the Blackburn office staff who help me keep on top of my correspondence.

After training I pick up Lainya's birthday present – a pair of diamond earrings.

I make a point of watching *Panorama* tonight because there's been a lot of advance publicity about the programme's investigations into Terry Venables and his business dealings. I must admit I don't understand a lot of it. You'd have to be an expert on company law to work out the allegations that are being made. But I take the view that whatever has happened in the England manager's business life, it makes no difference to his ability to do his football job.

NOVEMBER 1994

TUESDAY 1ST

Lainya's birthday. She loves the earrings but unfortunately I am not able to spend a great deal of time with her. I leave home at ten o'clock for training and get home for a couple of hours in the afternoon before leaving for tomorrow's game against Sheffield Wednesday. Footballers' wives have to be very understanding. There are many times, because of the requirements of the job, when we cannot be with them for family occasions like birthdays and Christmas, so we have to try to compensate and make up for lost time whenever we can.

We arrive at our hotel in Sheffield to discover that Newcastle have gone out of the UEFA Cup in Bilbao. Then Aston Villa lose on the away goals rule to the Turkish team Trabzonspor. Not a good night for English football.

WEDNESDAY 2ND

We train at Sheffield United's training ground and I discover I have left my kit at home. It's an unwritten rule that we all have to take our own training gear home and wash it – or at least our wives do. Fortunately I am able to borrow Stuart Ripley's because he never joins in training on a matchday. The match at Hillsborough is not a classic and certainly not one of our best performances of the season. I manage to grab the only goal of the game and although we are a little bit fortunate to win we are now accumulating points at a healthy rate. We have to accept that we are not going to go through the whole season playing pretty football. There are times when we have to dig in and the mark of a successful side is one which can win some games without playing outstandingly well.

THURSDAY 3RD

We arrive at the ground for training to discover that rumours of a trip to Spain next week for a game against Barcelona have been confirmed. There are mixed feelings about it, but on the positive side it could offer us a relaxing break in the sun with maybe a couple of rounds of golf.

Back home in the afternoon, we take Chloe to Children's World to do some of our Christmas shopping. Because Lainya is due to give birth in early December we are having to shop early this year.

In the evening I travel with Mike Newell to watch him play for the reserves against Stoke. When I was injured at the start of last season, Mike gave me a lot of moral support, especially when I began my comeback. I'm glad to return the favour now. We lose 2-0 but, with another 90 minutes under his belt, Mike will soon be back in the first team picture.

SATURDAY 5TH

Spurs are the visitors today with their caretaker manager Steve Perryman in charge after the sacking of Ossie Ardiles earlier in the week. You are always a bit wary of opponents in this situation. They can either be totally fired up and play with bags of spirit or be down in the dumps because of the upheavals which have taken place. Spurs never trouble us, to be honest, and you can tell that the events of the past few days are weighing heavily on their players. Jason Wilcox gives us the lead and I score a second after Justin Edinburgh brings me down in the box. You cannot help but feel a bit sorry for Tottenham but I reckon they have too many good players to go down. Mind you, that's been said about a few teams in the past and proved to be the kiss of death.

In the dressing room, Mike Newell winds Tim Flowers up by telling him he and his wife can't go to their bonfire party tonight because Catherine has agreed to go to one at her mother's. I know Tim and Jane have gone to a lot of trouble to prepare food for our three families so his face is a picture of despair – until Mike lets on he is only joking. We have a fun time with the fireworks – at least the three men do. The kids seem more interested in playing with their toys indoors and the women in chatting. So Tim, Mike and myself keep ourselves amused in the garden with the rockets and sparklers.

MONDAY 7TH

The getaway break to Spain turns out to be a nightmare. We leave home at 7.30 in the morning and arrive at our hotel in Almeria thirteen hours later. We have to fly from Manchester to Heathrow to Madrid (where there is a three-hour wait), before moving on to our final destination. To make matters worse, twelve of our kitbags go missing between Madrid and Almeria. The reason for the roundabout route is that clearance for the trip from the Football Association was late arriving and subsequently the direct flights to Almeira from Manchester could not accommodate us all.

I ring home to check on the England squad for the Nigeria game. The big news is that Chris Sutton has not been picked and that creates most of the media interest. There is no doubt that Chris has been showing international form since joining us from Norwich. As well as scoring goals consistently, he has pulled his weight for the benefit of the team as a whole. That is something you must do at Blackburn. There is no room for shirkers. No doubt Terry Venables has run the rule over all the in-form strikers this season and, in this particular position, the England manager seems spoiled for choice. I guess the same applies to Chris as to Andy Cole. All they can do is keep performing well and scoring goals for their clubs and I'm sure their chances will come.

TUESDAY 8TH

The nightmare continues. After a 45-minute journey to the ground where we are scheduled to train, we find the coach is too big to get down the narrow roadway. We all have to pile off and walk for one-and-a-half miles to the pitch. We expect Jeremy Beadle to appear at any minute. It's hardly worth it when we get there. The pitch is bumpy and downright dangerous so training is abandoned very quickly. The only thing left for us to do is head back to the hotel for an afternoon rest.

When I get to the ground for the game against Barcelona I find my match boots have been stolen. Tony Parkes had earlier laid out all the kit and locked the dressing-room door, but an intruder has somehow found a way in. I play in a spare pair which don't seem to do me any harm because I score twice in a 3-1 win. Barcelona have most of their star names playing, including Romario, Koeman and Bakero, so it's a good workout for us. The game is part of a mutual arrangement with the Spaniards who are due to pay us a return visit at the start of next season for the official opening of the new-look Ewood Park. We are pleased with our performance but after the problems of the trip we can't wait to travel home tomorrow.

WEDNESDAY 9TH

Up at 8.00 a.m. for the trip back. It's not too bad this time – only twelve hours door to door. At Heathrow airport there's a feeling of disbelief among the lads when we pick up the English newspapers and read about the bribery allegations concerning Bruce Grobbelaar. He's accused of taking backhanders to fix matches. I find it all hard to comprehend. I've certainly never heard of anything like this going on in our game. I prefer to reserve judgement on the Grobbelaar affair until I've heard all sides of the argument.

I collapse into bed at 9.30 p.m. absolutely shattered. I think this is the first time I've been to Spain and returned home jet-lagged.

THURSDAY 10TH

I'm off on my travels again today, heading south to link up with the England squad at Burnham Beeches for the Nigeria match.

Lainya's mum has arrived to stay with her while I'm away. With the birth getting closer, it's important she has someone to keep a close eye on her.

I meet my agent Tony Stephens on the M6 and then further down the motorway we pick up David Platt. We call in at Tony's house and meet Margaret, a grandmother, who is David's number one fan and has 58 scrapbooks of his career. David is writing his autobiography and wants to borrow the scrapbooks for the next few days. Apparently, Margaret's daughter-in-law has started an Alan Shearer collection – but mine is only up to two scrapbooks at this stage.

We move on to join the rest of the squad and have a brief meeting about the schedule for the next few days before retiring to bed.

FRIDAY 11TH

We start training at 9.45 and the morning session is taken up mostly with defensive work. It is not just restricted to the defenders. One of the criticisms from the Romanian game is that we didn't defend well enough from the front. So the emphasis today is to make sure the attackers close down the opposition as quickly as possible. In the afternoon there is a meeting of the England players' committee with the Football Association's chief executive Graham Kelly and commercial director Trevor Phillips. I was elected to the committee after the retirement of Gary Lineker from international football. Tony Adams, David Platt and Stuart Pearce are the other members. Today's meeting is to discuss the distribution of the commercial funds which are collected into the players' pool over the season from sponsorships, advertising and personal appearances. Those who have been in all the squads obviously get the larger shares but even those who are selected once or twice get a slice of the fund. This is one of the perks of playing for England and offers a nice financial bonus.

Having said that, I would play for England just for the honour and I'm sure that most of the lads feel the same way.

SATURDAY 12TH

A 9.30 start in the training ground because we have the option of travelling home at midday. I said I wouldn't make the journey again after the traffic problems last time, but it's important to spend some time with Lainya.

Paul, the Blackburn coach driver, takes Neil Ruddock and myself back home while Tim goes in a different car to his parents' home in the Midlands. Some people wonder whether it's really worthwhile joining up with the squad on a Thursday night only to disperse again on Saturday lunchtime. Terry Venables argues that every hour spent with his players is crucial. He sees so little of us during the course of a season that he can't afford to miss any opportunity to bring us together. I seem to have spent so little time at home recently I'm glad to make the effort to travel back and see my wife and daughter.

SUNDAY 13TH

Paul picks Neil and myself up at 4 p.m. and we collect David at Crewe and Tim at Coventry. We arrive at Burnham Beeches at 9 p.m. and settle down for an early night.

MONDAY 14TH

There has been more speculation in recent weeks about David Platt coming home from Italy. The news leaked out that he was buying a plot of land in Cheshire to build a new house and, of course, people put two and two together and came up with the answer that he was preparing for his return to England. I've discussed it with him and his explanation is that he's merely planning for his future. It's going to take at least eighteen months for the house to be built and I know David is more than happy to stay in Italy until he feels the time is right to return home. When he eventually does, there is a strong case for him to be regarded as our most successful export to Italy. He seems to have taken it all in his stride and mapped out his career over there with great care and attention to detail. David began at Bari – not one of the biggest clubs, but one which gave him the chance to acclimatise to the football and way of life away from the glare of publicity which Paul Gascoigne had to suffer. David played so well and made such an impact in a struggling side that the big guns came looking for him.

They do not come much bigger than his next club, Juventus. When it was time to move on from there, another top outfit wanted him and he has made his mark with Sampdoria where he will be staying for at least another year. Fame and fortune have come his way in Italy and few people would begrudge him that. He deserves everything because he has worked so hard for it. At the time of writing, David has scored more goals in Italy than any other British 'export' apart from John Charles – a phenomenal achievement for a midfield player.

TUESDAY 15TH

The team is announced before training. Tim Flowers is thrilled to be given another chance in goal and Neil is, likewise, absolutely delighted to win his first cap. Both deserve their selections. Tim has been in superb form for Blackburn and Neil is one of the main reasons why Liverpool have started to become a real force again. Because Tony Adams and Gary Pallister are both injured there is a new pairing at the back with Newcastle's Steve Howey partnering Neil. There is controversy over the selection of Dennis Wise ahead of Matthew Le Tissier but Terry Venables doesn't appear to be the type of manager who lets the Press pick his teams for him.

After training we spend a lazy evening watching the Under 21s beat the Republic of Ireland in front of a record crowd of 26,000 at Newcastle.

WEDNESDAY 16TH

We work on set pieces in training and in the afternoon I have to sort out my match tickets. For the first time my grandmother (my dad's mum) is coming to watch me play. She has only seen me in action on television before, so Mum and Dad are bringing her down to stay at the Wembley Hilton where we have managed to arrange a suite for her.

Considering there are a number of new caps in the side, our performance against a very exciting Nigerian team is good. Tim keeps us in the game with a couple of early saves and David Platt gives us the lead just before half time with a fine header. I have a shot well saved in the first half and miss a good opportunity after breaking clear of the offside trap. A diving header at goal towards the end earns me a kick on the head, quite near to the spot where I had the lump removed, but it isn't too painful. All in all, I feel it's one of my best performances for England, though I am replaced towards the end along with Peter Beardsley to give Teddy Sheringham and Matt Le Tissier a brief outing.

I meet the family afterwards and my grandmother tells me she has thoroughly enjoyed the game, though she does wonder whether she is an unlucky omen for me because I failed to score. On the way home we have to ring Kenny Dalglish to let him know that Tim, Graeme Le Saux and myself have come through unscathed and will be in for training tomorrow. I suspect that he just wants to check we're not in Stringfellows!

THURSDAY 17TH

Another day of travelling ahead. We haven't won or even taken a point from Ipswich in seven visits so the boss has decided we'll have a change of routine and make the long trip to East Anglia two days before the game. First we train and have our first full use of our new training facilities, complete with showers, sauna and jacuzzi. The journey to Ipswich takes five-and-a-half hours so there's little to do when we get there except retire for the night. Now that Mike Newell's back in the first team squad, he's taken over from Tim as my room-mate. He is not such a good manservant. He makes me a cup of tea in the morning, but doesn't get up for breakfast, so I have to do without my corn-flakes.

FRIDAY 18TH

I grab a piece of toast and a cuppa before training and someone points out an article by Bob Driscoll in the *Daily Star*. He has had a right go at me and tells Terry Venables I need a boot up the backside for strolling around Wembley on Wednesday night as if the England shirt was my own personal property. I think it's a bit harsh. I don't think anyone can ever accuse me of being complacent. I have never considered I have a divine right to wear any football shirt – certainly not an England one.

As I mentioned earlier, I believe I had one of my best international games. Still, it gives the other lads a chance to poke a bit of fun at me. Interestingly, the *Sun* reporter at the Wembley game awarded me seven out of ten for 'another class performance' while the *Star* marked me a four and described my display as 'dreadful'. You can't please everyone.

Press criticism is part and parcel of the game and when someone has a go it is best not to over-react. It irritates rather than angers me to read a report like the one written by Mr Driscoll. You ask why someone who has probably not played the game at a very high level should have the right to criticise you, but as we are always told, football is a game of opinions and so I suppose he is entitled to say what he likes. The *Star* article is the worst thing I have ever had written about me. I can handle criticism and will be the first to hold up my hands if I feel I have played poorly. But one thing you cannot throw at me is that I do not care or do not try.

After training we have a team meeting to discuss the new training ground and the need to treat the facilities with respect. One plus point for the players is that new laundry facilities will be made available which means we won't have to wash our own kits anymore.

It will be nice to have a place we can call our own to use each day. In the past we have used school pitches or any available piece of grass in the immediate area around Blackburn. Our least favourite was a place called Pleasington where a road runs alongside the pitches towards a crematorium. Our sessions were often interrupted by funeral processions during which we would stop training and stand still and silent to show our respect for the deceased and bereaved.

SATURDAY 19TH

I enjoy my lie-in today after all the hectic travelling recently. We have to make a couple of changes for the Ipswich game with Henning Berg and Jason Wilcox suspended. We seem to cope well enough and Chris Sutton scores the first goal from my headed pass. But if it hadn't been for Tim's saves we would be behind at half-time. We receive a telling off from the boss at half-time which is thoroughly deserved but we roll up our sleeves and perform much better in the second half.

It is unusual for the manager and Ray Harford to blow their tops but, when the occasion warrants it, they do not hold back. You never find any teacups flying around or temper tantrums – time is limited during half-time and they use it to get across their constructive criticism, clearly and effectively.

Chris returns the favour for me and I score with a tap-in and Tim Sherwood adds a third to give us a comfortable 3-1 win. That's five wins on the trot now since we lost against Manchester United. It's beginning to look very interesting at the top, where United have taken over from Newcastle who lost today at Wimbledon. It leaves us just a couple of points behind the leaders, whereas this time a year ago there was a fifteen point gap between us.

There is an unstated but growing feeling that this could be our year.

MONDAY 21ST

A day off so after taking Lainya's mum to the airport for a flight back to Southampton, we do some more Christmas shopping before returning home. In the evening I watch the Liverpool-Everton game on TV. It's Joe Royle's first match since taking over at Goodison and having played for him when he was in charge of the England Under 21s, I know what a good choice he is as their new manager. A 2-0 win for Everton over the old enemy is the best start imaginable for Joe and I'm certain he'll turn things around for them.

I was grateful to him for helping me to adjust to the demands of international football with the Under 21s. As a former international striker himself, he knew what he was talking about and it was a valuable part of my football education. I scored thirteen goals in twelve games at this level and I was able to push my claims and progress towards the senior squad. Being called up for an international side at this age reminded me of my trial days at Southampton. You know you are a reasonable player in your own surroundings but suddenly you find yourself thrown in among the best talent in your age group from all around the country. The important thing to remember is that the chance to shine might not come along again, so you have to grab it with both hands. Part of the challenge is learning to play alongside relative strangers when you only have two or three days to adjust to their styles.

I was fortunate to make a good, early impression at every international stage. I scored on my debut for the England Under 17s against the Republic of Ireland, in my first match for the Under 21s against the same country and on my first appearance for the senior side against France.

TUESDAY 22ND

Quite a hard morning at the new training ground with and without the ball. I'm sitting in the restaurant afterwards when the receptionist, Susan, comes over to me and tells me that two CID officers want to see me. In a situation like this, you automatically fear the worst. My first thought is that something has happened to Lainya at home. My fears are unfounded. It turns out that a man has been arrested for making nuisance phone calls and he has obtained the ex-directory numbers and the addresses of Colin Hendry and myself. Apparently he was able to acquire them because his sister works for British Telecom. Colin has recently changed his number because of the amount of strange calls he's been getting. Having been away from home so much in the last couple of weeks, I haven't been aware of any problem on our phone but a check with Lainya when I get home puts my mind at rest. The man is being held in custody so we can put the matter to the back of our minds.

During the afternoon I do an interview with the *News of the World* based around the fact that I'm facing Neil Ruddock in the Coca-Cola Cup tie against Liverpool next week. The theme of the article is the 'hard-men' defenders I have come up against. I make the point that I tend not to think of individual defenders so much now as defensive partnerships – like Tony Adams and Steve Bould (Arsenal), Darren Peacock and Steve Howey (Newcastle), Ugo Ehiogu and Paul McGrath (Aston Villa) and the triple barrier at Liverpool of Neil Ruddock, John Scales and Phil Babb.

If I had to single out one defender who has always made life difficult for me it would be Tony Adams. The Arsenal skipper is a hard man. When he tackles you from behind you feel it. As well as being strong on the ground, he is good in the air, organises his fellow defenders and refuses to accept defeat.

My idea of the perfect defender – and I hope such a species will never exist – would combine the best attributes of Adams, Des Walker and Neil Ruddock. If you added Tony's tackling, grit and determination to Des's pace and marking ability and Neil's power and passing ability (he insists he can open a can of beans with his left foot), you would have a real Frankenstein's monster – a striker's nightmare.

WEDNESDAY 23RD

No midweek game so another hard day's training. The new facilities are exceptionally good. The new restaurant and recreation area is a great place to relax and mingle with the other lads afterwards. It's something Kenny Dalglish is very keen to encourage because of the positive effect it has on team spirit. We work and play together so our manager reckons it's good for morale to sit down together afterwards for a bite to eat and a chat.

In the afternoon I go round to Chris Sutton's house because tonight we're switching on the Christmas lights in Blackburn town centre. Before the official ceremony at the Town Hall, I ask the Mayor and Mayoress of Blackburn if the lights have ever failed to work and they insist they haven't. Well, there's a first time for everything. Only half of them light up when we pull the switch but they all work at the second attempt. This must be the first time this season the partnership between Chris and myself hasn't sparked into life.

Back home in the evening I watch Manchester United's European Cup defeat in Gothenburg. It looks as if their campaign in Europe is going to end as dismally as ours but it's nothing that any follower of English football can find any pleasure in.

THURSDAY 24TH

Lainya visits the doctor and it seems the birth could be at any time now. All she can do is be patient and wait with her bag packed, ready to rush off to the hospital.

There's plenty of activity at the training ground today. We usually turn our thoughts of how we will cope with the opposition two days before a game. If we are up against a passing team, we concentrate on harrassing them into mistakes and, if they're a long ball team, we devote our attention to shutting down their lines of supply and winning the aerial battles. Ray Harford handles this side of training and he's very good at getting his points across effectively and in a way we can all understand. That's not a dig at the boss's Scottish accent. Honestly.

On the way home, Mike Newell and I take a look around a new golf course which is being built at Formby Hall. It's due to be opened in the autumn of next year. It's just around the corner from where we live so we both want to become members.

When I get home, I have to have a picture taken for the *News of the World* with Chloe and Neil Ruddock and his two children, Millie and Joshua. There is a mix-up over the times however. The arrangement was for half-past three but the photographer arrives at three and Neil doesn't turn up till four. There's just about enough light available for us to pose for the picture in the garden.

FRIDAY 25TH

There is a real buzz round the training ground. We know we're in the middle of a good run and are going into our matches feeling very confident. I stay behind when the session is over to practise a few penalties. We haven't been awarded one for a few weeks and I want to be sure I don't slip up. Without a keeper between the posts, I strike the ball into a chosen corner of the net. It's easy when there's no one trying to stop it.

There's another big shock on the sports pages today with an admission by Arsenal's Paul Merson that he has a cocaine habit. I find it unbelievable, having known Paul for a few years from the England squad. Earlier this season there was an article by Mark Dennis, claiming that the game was full of players taking drugs. I'd dismissed that as a load of rubbish but now this Merson story has made everyone wonder how widespread it could be. I just feel very sad that Paul has allowed himself and his club to be dragged down in this way.

Naturally there are temptations for young men earning a lot of money and living a glamorous lifestyle, but you have to be strong enough and sensible enough to say 'no'. There are so many hangers-on around the game these days and among them are sure to be some who see football as a market to peddle their drugs. I have never seen or heard of any drug dealings within football, nor do I want to. I wouldn't go within a hundred miles of the stuff. Interestingly, I made that video for the players' union recently, warning of the perils of drug abuse but that was aimed at young trainees – not seasoned professionals.

The Children In Need appeal is on BBC television tonight and, on the way home from training, I say to Mike Newell that I'll have my head shaved if he pledges £1,000. I watch the box nervously but, much to my relief, he doesn't take up the challenge.

SATURDAY 26TH

We didn't have a particularly good night's sleep because Chloe is restless, but I have a lie-in until around eleven and feel pretty good as I set off for the ground for the game against Queen's Park Rangers. Henning Berg returns after suspension and is brought into the centre of the defence to help cope with Les Ferdinand's pace and power.

We get off to a great start with Chris Sutton scoring helped by a deflection off Karl Ready. It's funny how, when things start going your way, you get little breaks like that. A month ago we were on the receiving end of all the unlucky bounces and deflections but, they reckon over the course of a season, they tend to balance themselves out. I get our second after the interval when I put the ball into the net despite being pushed and pulled all over the place by Ready. The referee Joe Worrall reckons he would have awarded a penalty even if I hadn't scored, so it is encouraging to see an official make good use of the advantage rule.

We are awarded a penalty soon afterwards for a foul on Stuart Ripley. Yesterday's practice pays off as I play it in exactly the right spot. Then another chance comes my way. I am 30 yards out and Robbie Slater is screaming for the ball out on the right. We are three goals up and it's my chance for a hat-trick, so I give it a go. In different circumstances I would have probably laid it off. I hit it just right and the ball flies in off the underside of the bar. It's probably the best goal of my career – but one of those which either sails over the stand or hits the back of the net. This is the third hat-trick of my League career. My first came on my debut for Southampton as a seventeen year old and the second in the 3-3 draw at Leeds last season. This is my first at Ewood Park so I'm especially proud of it. I collect the match ball afterwards and get the other lads to sign it. It will fit nicely in my trophy room at home, not that there's too much in it – yet.

Spirits are really high in the dressing-room when we learn that Manchester United have been held by Arsenal and we are top of the table for the first time in two years. But once the initial euphoria dies down, the realisation sets in that no medals are handed out for being in top spot at this stage in the season. No one needs to remind us that we have to keep on doing the things which got us there or we'll soon be toppled.

I round off a perfect day with a meal at home with Lainya and another look at my goals on *Match of the Day*.

SUNDAY 27TH

We go for a morning walk on the beach but I make sure we're back at midday so I can see my goals yet again on the Sky TV football round-up. I keep expecting the third one to fly over the bar but it always ends up bang on target! There's not a single word of my interview about central defenders in the *News of the World*. It must have got lost among all the Paul Merson follow-up stories.

MONDAY 28TH

I ring Neil Ruddock before leaving for training to congratulate him on his own goal against Spurs on Saturday. His wife says he's asleep and she doesn't want to disturb him. A likely story. I manage to get through to him when I return home in the afternoon and he tells me the goal was one of his worst moments in football. I'm careful not to upset him too much because he's marking me on Wednesday night.

TUESDAY 29TH

A light workout in training before returning home to rest before tomorrow's big game with Liverpool. Lainya feels a few twinges but it turns out to be a false alarm.

WEDNESDAY 30TH

I travel in early with Tim and Mike and, after some shooting practice, we call it a day. We check into the hotel in the afternoon and discover that Liverpool are staying there as well. When Mike and I settle down for an afternoon nap we are disturbed by two telephone calls. There is no one on the other end but we can guess who it is. After the second one we leave it off the hook.

We start the game in a very positive manner and are unlucky when Stuart Ripley's shot hits the bar. Liverpool take the lead with a tremendous strike from Ian Rush which no keeper in the world would have saved. That proves to be an ominous sign. The Welsh striker goes on to complete a superb hat-trick and although Chris Sutton pulls one back the game is well beyond our reach. The defeat is hard enough to swallow but an incident occurs in the second half which really sours the occasion for me. With the score at 2-0 I chase a ball chipped over the top of their defence and am clean through with only David James ahead of me. I am tackled by John Scales and Neil Ruddock. When I'm down on the floor Neil tramples all over me. He could have avoided me.

I am so angry that I stand up and grab him around the throat. He tries to push me away. The referee Roger Dilkes is quickly on the scene and we both offer our view of what happened. I point out that I was through on goal and was brought down. Neil claims I dived. The ref insists he could send us both off for raising our hands to each other but settles for a yellow card apiece. That's my third caution of the season and I'm now on twelve disciplinary points so I'd better stay out of trouble. But I was so angry at being trodden on, it was just an instinctive reaction. I go up to the players' lounge afterwards but don't see Neil. Nor do I want to. I calm down a bit but get home feeling pretty dejected. I have a very sleepless night tossing and turning and playing the events of the match over and over again in my mind.

DECEMBER 1994

THURSDAY 1ST

The baby is officially due today but as there are no signs of an arrival, I report for training, have a quick massage and go straight back home. All the newspapers have pictures of me with my hands round Neil's throat. I have a quick chuckle about it and Neil rings me up later. I ask him, 'Are you ringing to apologise?' He replies, 'No, I am not.' He laughs and says he thought he was going to get sent off for the tackle, so he decided he would go off in style by walking all over me. I'm not sure whether he's being serious but we agree it's an incident best forgotten. There is no sign of the baby but a visit to the hospital confirms it could be here at any moment.

FRIDAY 2ND

I collect my newspapers from the postbox at the end of the drive and am surprised to see Neil and the Liverpool manager Roy Evans are having a go at me. They claim I get away with murder by backing into defenders and pushing them all over the place, whereas defenders are being punished by referees for far less. My view is that if these two are having a good old moan about me I must be doing something right. Interestingly there's a League table published of the worst offenders of recent years and Neil is in second place with over 130 disciplinary points. I must pull his leg about this sometime.

We travel to London this morning for tomorrow's game against Wimbledon and train when we get there. I must admit my mind is on my wife and the forthcoming birth of our second child. Her mum and dad have travelled up to be with her but I want to be there when the baby is born. I mention this to Ray Harford and he tells me that it's entirely up to me. If something happens today I can get back home quickly and maybe return to London for the game. I wait by the phone but the only call I get is from Tony Stephens who tells me he has heard that there'll be more speculation about me moving to Italy in tomorrow's newspapers.

SATURDAY 3RD

The headlines claim that my value is now up to £12 million and that Inter Milan want to swap Dennis Bergkamp for me, although Sampdoria and Napoli are also supposed to be in the running as well. All very flattering but I take it with the usual heap of salt. Whatever happened to my Italian lessons?

Now I have to concentrate my thoughts on the game, though I make one last call to Lainya to make sure everything is all right at home. Wimbledon will not be the easiest of opponents. A couple of seasons ago we were stuffed 4-2 by them when a victory would have taken us to the top of the League, so we have to be on full alert. After a scrappy, goalless first half we take control after the break. Goals from Mark Atkins, Jason Wilcox and myself give us victory and confirm our position as League leaders. I am one of the first on the coach for the journey home and I ring Lainya to discover, to my amazement, that she has gone out shopping with her parents. I call back again at 9.00 p.m. and they have all gone out for a meal. When I arrive at 10.30 p.m. I am half expecting to discover she has gone out to a nightclub. Of course, she's there with her feet up and, while I stay up to watch *Match of the Day*, she goes to bed.

SUNDAY 4TH

It's three in the morning before I get to sleep but I'm woken at half-past five by Lainya telling me it's time to go to hospital. I'm walking around like a half-dead donkey but I manage to compose myself and ring the hospital to tell them we're on the way. Lainya's parents look after Chloe while we head off to the maternity ward. I remember how I struggled to cope and felt queasy when Chloe was born, but I am determined to witness the birth. At precisely 11.57 a.m. our second daughter arrives into the world. I didn't think it would be so emotional but there are tears all round again. The baby weighs in at 8 lb 5 oz. In our deliberations beforehand, we were certain it was going to be a girl and thought about calling her Bethany. But we have always liked the name Hollie and feel it would be very appropriate at this time of year. I am despatched to the nearest telephone and spend around £50 ringing all our family and friends to tell them the good news. Chloe visits this afternoon and is very excited. Her favourite dolly is called Molly and now she has a sister called Hollie. I can see it is all going to be very confusing. I leave the hospital at around eleven and go straight to bed for a welcome night's sleep.

MONDAY 5TH

A quick glance at the newspapers finds me grabbing the headlines again with a story on the back pages that I have a clause in my Blackburn contract restricting my transfer fee to £5 million. It is absolute nonsense but I have more important things on my mind than this. I pick up some flowers for Lainya and a teddy for Hollie on my way to hospital. Lainya has suffered a slight complication which means she has to stay in hospital for an extra day or two but she is coping extremely well.

I start to reminisce about Lainya and myself. We've been together for eight years now. We met at a wine bar in Southampton, having been introduced by a young apprentice called Paul Masters who used to clean my boots at The Dell. He was going out with Lainya's sister and arranged for me to meet her. We got on immediately. She was my first serious girlfriend and we went out for around three years before we decided to get married.

Although we did not plan it, we lived together before we were married. We were looking round for a house and found a two-bedroomed semi-detached which cost us £67,500 and decided to move in virtually straightaway. We had a big wedding with loads of family and friends as guests and spent three glorious weeks in Jamaica on our honeymoon.

When I was given a new contract, we decided to move up the housing market and bought a four-bedroomed detached about a mile away from our first home and stayed there until the move to Blackburn came along.

I spend most of today with Lainya but have to leave her in the evening to attend a Variety Club dinner where I am due to collect the award as the north-west sports personality of the year. The Variety Club do so much good work for children's charities and I don't want to let them down, but I contact them in advance and tell them I will only be able to turn up for the presentation. I dash home from the hospital to change and am picked up by car to go to the hotel. I enter a room full of 900 people all wearing dinner suits. I apologise for wearing a lounge suit and also for my lightning visit but everyone understands that I have had other things to occupy my time.

TUESDAY 6TH

Back in training and it's a hard day's work with not a ball in sight. I am struggling a bit because of my lack of sleep. I don't hang around for too long after training because Lainya and the baby are coming home today. There's a great feeling of excitement around the house and Chloe is very proud of her new sister. Amid all this I get a phone call telling me that Chris Sutton and myself have jointly won the Carling Player of the Month award and that Kenny Dalglish is Manager of the Month. Then the *Daily Star* calls to tell me I have been voted their Star Man of the Month. I find the latter award strange in view of the criticism I got from one of their writers after the last England game. Our first night at home with Hollie isn't too much of an ordeal, though Chloe is awake at 4.00 a.m. and we all get up in the morning feeling totally exhausted.

FRIDAY 9TH

Before training Chris Sutton and I have to pose for a picture with our Carling awards and the sponsors have provided a saw and the trophy cut in half for the purposes of the photograph. Then, before we start work, our goalkeeping coach Terry Gennoe comes in with a young lad of ten who has suffered three fractures of the skull in an accident. It makes his day to meet all the lads and when I discover I am his favourite player I give him a pair of my old match boots and his face is a picture. His eyes fill up with tears and he is totally lost for words. Back home in the afternoon, the baby faces her first photo session for the *News of the World* with myself, Lainya, Chloe and Molly. Because it's Friday night, I head for the spare bedroom and manage a good eleven or twelve hours' sleep.

SATURDAY 10TH

I wake up feeling absolutely dreadful, probably because I've had too much sleep. Before the start of today's home game against Southampton, I feel in the worst physical state I have been in for a long, long time. I am tired and lethargic and, interestingly enough, quite a few of my team-mates remark that they feel the same. A tremendous strike from Mark Atkins gives us an early lead and five minutes later Richard Hall pulls me down in the penalty box. I have only missed one from the spot this season – on the opening day when Bruce Grobbelaar saved it. I decided before the game that if we are awarded one today I will put it in the opposite corner – wide of his left hand.

Bruce outguesses me and makes a fine stop but, fortunately, the ball comes back out to me and I score from the rebound. Southampton have come with a heavily reinforced defence with a sweeper in front and one behind their back four. So we are pleased that we have broken them down so effectively.

We take our foot off the pedal which is a mistake because, after half-time, they adopt a more adventurous approach. Matt Le Tissier pulls one back and, even when I make it 3-1, the Saints refuse to lie down. Matt grabs a second goal and I will be very surprised if it's not the goal of the season. He beats two men and from about 25 yards he chips a shot which bends and dips into the top corner of the net. We are quite relieved when the final whistle comes. I wonder how much more difficult it would have been if Southampton had been more enterprising straight from the kick-off. I suppose we will have to get used to teams coming to Ewood Park trying to smother us with negative tactics but the best solution is to get an early goal and make them come out at us. I only hope they don't all do it as emphatically as Southampton, but they won't all have a player with the ability of Le Tissier to conjure up spectacular goals. Manchester United have won again and Newcastle are back on the winning trail with a 3-1 victory over Leicester City so they are still breathing down our necks at the top of the table.

SUNDAY 11TH

It was my turn on baby feeding duty last night (just as well she's not being breast fed) because I never sleep too much after a game. I am up early to pack my bags to catch a flight from Manchester to Heathrow because I have been invited to the BBC Sports Personality of the Year presentations. Mike Newell accompanies me. We watch Crystal Palace hold Liverpool to a 0-0 draw in the live TV game which is a good result for us because it means the men from Anfield have slipped further behind us.

The BBC awards night is being held at the Queen Elizabeth Conference Centre and I am asked to sit among an illustrious group of celebrities – Chris Eubank, fresh from his victory over Henry Wharton the previous night, Stephen Hendry and Damon Hill. I get a mention – a reference to me being worth £12 million which goes to show how much people believe what they read in the newspapers. The main award goes to Damon Hill which surprises me a bit. I thought it would go to one of the athletes – Sally Gunnell, Linford Christie or Colin Jackson – because they finished the year with another bucketful of gold medals between them. Damon put up a tremendous fight for the Formula One world title but only finished runner-up. But I don't mean to underplay his achievement because he competes in one of the most hazardous of all sports. I wouldn't mind having a spin for fun, but I wouldn't fancy making a living from motor racing.

There is a buffet and a few drinks afterwards and I spent some time with the Wigan Rugby League team. I chat to Phil Clarke, who is the Great Britain vice-captain, and he invites me to his sports medicine centre to discuss my diet. It's quite late before we get to bed but Kenny Dalglish has already told us we have to be back in Blackburn for training the next morning. He is staying behind in London to do some Christmas shopping with his wife.

MONDAY 12TH

We are up at seven o'clock and the thought of the gaffer having a lie-in is too much of a temptation. We ring his room at 7.20 and it takes him a long time to pick the phone up, so we know he was fast asleep. We hang up without saying anything and make a dash for the airport. Not that we need to be in a hurry. The flight is delayed and we don't arrive in Manchester till 10.45. We have to be in training at eleven o'clock and I do my impersonation of Damon Hill to get us to the training ground. We are still ten minutes late. It's the first time in my life I have not been in on time. Unlike at most clubs, there are no fines handed out for being late. The gaffer trusts us to be punctual and no one takes advantage of it.

The good news is that we are given a couple of days off. I was not the only one to feel a bit leg-weary on Saturday, so the management feel two days without training will benefit us. No one argues and I dash home and fall asleep in front of the television.

TUESDAY 13TH

A lazy day. I take the dog for a walk and think about going to watch my colleagues Chris Sutton, Tim Sherwood and Jason Wilcox play for the England B team against the Republic of Ireland at Anfield. But it's such a filthy night I decide to stay at home and watch it on TV. Andy Cole and Chris Sutton do quite well up front. Andy and substitute Robbie Fowler get the goals in a 2-0 win.

WEDNESDAY 14TH

Something very unusual happens today. For the first time in about five years I hand-wash and hoover the cars. It's not like me to be this industrious and I immediately regret it because it's freezing cold. I'll stick to the car wash in future. The big news outside sport at the moment is that some lucky person has won over £17 million on the national lottery. Apparently, it's a family from Blackburn who want to remain anonymous. But as further information leaks out it emerges that they live in a two-bedroomed terrace house and the father works in a factory. So there's no point in sending begging letters to any of my team-mates.

I buy my lottery tickets each week using the same numbers chosen from family birthdays. My sister finds it strange that someone as well off as me should try to win the big prize but I have told her that, if my numbers come up, the cash will go to our mum.

SATURDAY 17TH

We travelled to Leicester overnight for today's game at Filbert Street and we know we are in for a tough game because it's their first game under Mark McGhee who has moved from Reading to take over from Brian Little as manager. Sure enough Leicester prove a hard nut to crack. They seem intent on making it difficult for us to play and become only the third team this season to prevent us from scoring. A goalless draw is the fairly predictable outcome, though we feel we might have pinched victory if two chances which fell to Chris Sutton had gone in. The first, a diving header from my cross, is superbly saved by Kevin Poole and Chris puts the second high over the bar from my knock-down. Mark McGhee says afterwards that he had gone into the match with a gameplan to stop Chris and myself. He argues that, by keeping us quiet, Blackburn's effectiveness as a team is massively reduced. I suppose the statistics support that argument since the pair of us have been on target so regularly but no one at the club pretends we are a two-man outfit. Chris and I are quick to appreciate that without a prompt and accurate supply from the flanks and midfield we would be less prolific. We return to the dressing-room to learn that Manchester United have lost to Nottingham Forest and Newcastle have been held by Coventry, so it has been a satisfying day's work for us.

It's my turn for chauffeuring duty from the M6. Tim is the first to be dropped off and I give him a toot on my car horn as I drive away from his home. That starts a debate between Mike and myself about whether it's legal to do that after 9.00 p.m. I argue that it is and claim that I know the Highway Code off by heart. The words have hardly left my lips when I notice a flashing blue light in my rear view mirror. It's hard to believe this – but we are in the same road and outside virtually the same house where I was stopped and given a speeding ticket recently.

Fortunately the policeman is a bit more understanding this time, though Mike does his best to cause confusion by turning the radio up full blast as the officer approaches my vehicle. First he wants to know why I didn't score against Leicester and then asks if I know how fast I had been travelling in the 30 mph area. I reply: 'Was it between 30 and 35?' He beckons me over and points out the reading which shows 50.1 mph. I'm convinced I'm in for another fine and more penalty points but the officer is kind enough to let me off with a caution. I drive home cautiously and thank my lucky stars that my policewoman friend who booked me for doing 42 mph is not patrolling the area tonight. But I really have to be more responsible about my speeding and realise I am not a budding Damon Hill.

SUNDAY 18TH

It's the club's Christmas party and Lainya and I arrange a babysitter for our first night out for a long time. It's a pleasant

Daddy's girl: my eldest daughter Chloe has brought great joy to the family and helps me escape the pressures of football (*News of the World*)

Right: What a headache. Defeat against Trelleborg in the UEFA Cup leaves me feeling at an all-time low (*Action Images*)

Below: I had to dash straight from hospital the night after Hollie had been born, to pick up the Variety Club's north-west sports personality award from Graeme Souness (*Jim Harvey*)

bove: Friends and neighbours. I
njoy a laugh with Neil Ruddock
against Liverpool . . .

. but the joking stops as we get to
ips with each other after our flare-
up (*News of the World/The Sun*)

My England team-mate David Platt has become a role model for any young playe (*The Sun*)

Below: The SAS strike again. Chris Sutt made a tremendous impact after his £5 million transfer from Norwich, and we h it off immediately as partners (*News of the World*)

he first team picture of the Shearers at Christmas. Baby Hollie (born 4 December) seems unimpressed by the fuss and carries on sleeping (*News of the World*)

There are few prouder days in my life than when I pull on my international shirt and turn out for my country (*The Sun*)

The 100th League goal of my career flies past Kevin Hitchcock of Chelsea (*Simon Wilkinson/Varley-Wilkinson*)

Above: Chris Sutton and myself with the
remiership trophy, medals and wide grins at
Anfield (*Lancashire Evening Telegraph*)

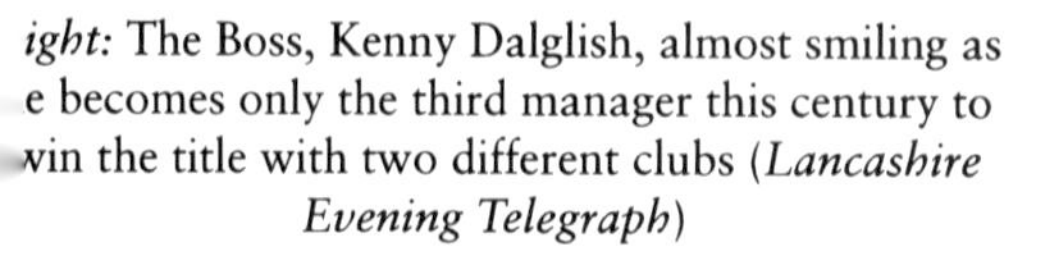
ight: The Boss, Kenny Dalglish, almost smiling as
e becomes only the third manager this century to
vin the title with two different clubs (*Lancashire
Evening Telegraph*)

Relief, jubilation and a lot of laughs as we pose in front of the Kop
(*Lancashire Evening Telegraph*)

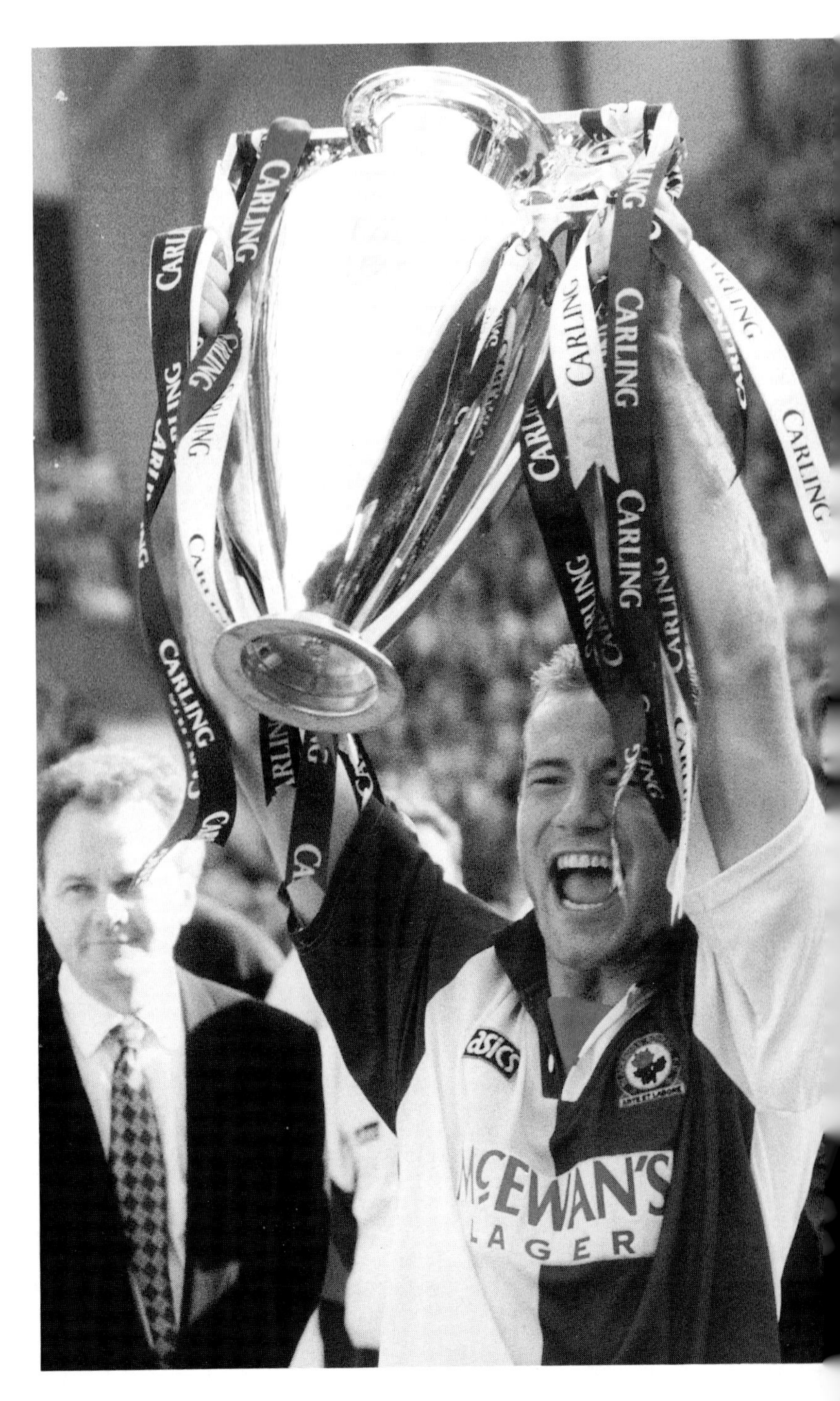

Proudest moment of my career so far. The first major trophy I've won, and the first that Blackburn have won in 81 years. Here's to many more (*Lancashire Evening Telegraph*)

evening and, though normally we would have stayed the night in the hotel, we have to be back to feed the baby at 2.00 a.m.

MONDAY 19TH

After training, it's time to give the apprentice who cleans my boots, Brett Ormerod, his Christmas box. I give him the choice of £30 in his hand or a bit of a gamble. He can choose to pick one of three cups, containing £1, £25 or £50. He decides to go for the cups and pockets the £50. As I'm feeling generous I spend the afternoon sorting out Lainya's Christmas present.

WEDNESDAY 21ST

The second of two days off. I have started to feel the strain of waking up in the middle of the night to feed the baby so I have a lie-in. In the afternoon we take Hollie out on her first shopping expedition and then have a family lunch in Southport.

THURSDAY 22ND

We know training will be tough today – our reward for having two rest days – and so it proves to be with some hard running and weights work. The boss is not at work. We receive a message saying he is suffering from gastroenteritis. We know he went out last night for an ex-Liverpool players' reunion, so it sounds a likely story. It's the Blackburn players' Christmas party and we head into Blackburn in the afternoon and visit a few pubs. One or two of the lads are a little the worse for wear but Tim and I are the sensible ones and we leave early. I arrive home at 9.00 p.m. and discover that Lainya has locked herself out of the house and has been at Neil and Sarah Ruddock's for the last three hours.

FRIDAY 23RD

There is a hard frost at the training ground so our workout is restricted to a jog and a brief session with the ball. Hollie has to pay her first visit to the doctor's because she has a cough and sticky eyes and is prescribed some antibiotics. Lainya's mum and dad arrive to spend Christmas and New Year with us.

SATURDAY 24TH

The training ground is still covered with frost but we manage to complete a fairly hectic session. The boss is not back at work so we guess there must be something wrong with him after all. I return home to find that the tumble drier has packed up so I go on a hasty visit to the shops for an early Christmas present for Lainya. Then we settle back for the evening to await the arrival of Santa Claus.

SUNDAY 25TH

For the third year since I joined Blackburn from Southampton, we have been given Christmas Day off. The boss has a young family of his own, so naturally he appreciates how special it is to be at home at this particular time. Apart from that, he trusts us not to overindulge with food and drink. We are all up at eight o'clock to see what Santa has brought us. Chloe spends most of the morning playing on her new rocking-horse but she is surrounded by new dolls, games, puzzles and books and doesn't know which to turn to first. I suppose we have spoiled her, but she'll have to make the most of it because she'll have competition from Hollie next year. I get some new clothes and an electronic gadget which enables me to video-record all my favourite TV programmes at the touch of a button. My present for Lainya is very well received – a diamond necklace to match the earrings I bought for her birthday. Once the presents are all opened, we settle down for Christmas lunch, superbly prepared by Lainya and her mum. Although I'm lucky that I don't put on weight very easily, I don't overdo it. I am careful with my diet as a rule and fortunately I enjoy all the things which are good for healthy living – like fish, pasta and potatoes. To blow the cobwebs away and stretch my legs, I take the dog for a long walk in the evening and then settle down for my normal eve-of-match routine and retire early to the spare bedroom to make sure I get some sleep.

MONDAY 26TH

Mike, Tim and I decide to go into the training ground an hour early to work off the Christmas pudding but when we get there the gates are locked and there isn't a soul in sight. We call Tony Parkes who has a set of keys. He lets us in and the extra activity does us a power of good. The big talking point is that Kenny Dalglish was admitted to hospital on Christmas Eve to have his appendix removed which means he will be missing from the scene for a few weeks. Without wishing to sound too unkind, we don't really miss him. The boss has got such a well-drilled routine and Ray Harford is such a capable number two that we just get on with things quite normally in preparation for tonight's game against Manchester City. I suppose that is a tribute in itself to the boss because he has instilled such a sense of responsibility and discipline into the club.

I give us a tenth-minute lead against City and Mark Atkins makes it 2-0 but we don't have it all our own way and, after Niall Quinn pulls one back, we are thankful to make it to half-time in front. After the break we assume full control and Graeme Le Saux rounds off the scoring to give us a comfortable win. Because we have a game on Wednesday we are whisked off to a hotel in Blackburn for the night. Inevitably, sleep is difficult after a game and many of us sit up into the small hours watching England take another battering in the Test Match in Australia.

TUESDAY 27TH

After a sauna at the training ground we are allowed to go home – and there is another Christmas feast being prepared in the Shearer household where we have been joined by Lainya's sister Shona and her fiancé Paul. It's a huge meal but there are no complaints from me because I love turkey and could eat it every day.

WEDNESDAY 28TH

We regroup in the hotel for the match against Leeds and are just leaving for the ground, smartly kitted out in collars and ties when one of the receptionists says, 'Mr Shearer, we have just heard the match has been postponed.' There has been so much rain recently, it's hardly surprising our pitch is waterlogged and we all head for home, rather disappointed because we are on such a good roll and look forward to every game with great anticipation. The mood in the camp is so buoyant that we are confident of taking on anyone and don't want our momentum interrupted. Our spirits are raised when we learn later in the evening that Manchester United have been held to a 1-1 draw at home by Leicester City, so, without even kicking a ball, our grip on the leadership is strengthened.

Back at home, we are all in the dark because of an electricity failure. It means I can't use my new video gadget to record *Match of the Day* but we make our own entertainment and play cards by candlelight.

THURSDAY 29TH

The weather is atrocious at the training ground, with a howling wind and driving rain making it very unpleasant. The session is called to a halt when one of the mobile goalposts is blown over and hits Tim Flowers on the head. I swear he never felt a thing and the crossbar suffered far more damage than he did.

SATURDAY 31ST

We travelled to south London overnight for the game against Crystal Palace and our match day lie-in is interrupted by a fire alarm going off at 7.45 a.m. The Blackburn lads are the last to assemble so it's just as well it's a false alarm or our title challenge would have gone up in flames. It's interesting to note that our defender Alan Wright appears immaculately groomed with his hair gelled down – heaven knows what he was doing up at that time in the morning. I manage to get back to sleep for a couple of hours when we return to our rooms but our performance in the afternoon is a pretty tired-looking affair. The pitch is heavy and the game is not much of a spectacle but on a day like this you are happy to chisel out a result. Tim Sherwood scores the only goal of the game and the news that Manchester United have been held again – this time at Southampton – means we are now three points clear at the top with a game in hand. I am home before midnight and Lainya and I see the New Year in quietly with a few glasses of wine.

JANUARY 1995

SUNDAY 1ST

We all have to report to the training ground and no one seems to be suffering with a hangover, though I don't feel too good myself. I can assure you my condition is not caused by too much alcohol. Despite all the care I took with my eating, I reckon I am suffering from an overdose of turkey and I'm glad to get home. It is not the ideal start to the year but, if 1995 carries on the way 1994 ended, I shall have no complaints.

MONDAY 2ND

I wake up with a headache and an upset stomach and am definitely not on top of the world as I travel in for the home game against West Ham. However, I am careful not to tell anyone that I feel under the weather. Can you imagine the stick I'd get if I told Ray Harford, 'I'm suffering with the trots today.' It's a case of grinning and getting on with it. Despite my delicate condition I score my second hat-trick of the season in a 4-2 victory over the Hammers, albeit with the help of two penalties. It makes me feel 100 per cent better but I don't hang around to celebrate. I go straight home to bed.

FRIDAY 6TH

I have been laid up in bed for the last three days, trying to shake off the effects of a stomach bug, so I am looking forward to getting back to work with the lads. First I have to help Lainya pack her bags and load the kids into the car for their journey up to the north-east. We are playing Newcastle in the third round of the FA Cup on Sunday and there is a Shearer family get-together which I will join after the game. I am left all on my own after training but for once I decide not to gatecrash any of my neighbours for dinner. Lainya has left me a ready-made pasta meal to pop into the microwave. It's delicious. I didn't realise cooking was so easy.

SATURDAY 7TH

We travel up to Newcastle after training and listen to the FA Cup reports on the radio. There are not too many shocks, apart from Wrexham's win over Ipswich. We arrive at around five o'clock and my dad looks in at the hotel for a half-hour chat before I retire to bed.

SUNDAY 8TH

Chris Sutton and I take a lot of stick from the Newcastle crowd before the game but it is something we have come to expect wherever we play now. We manage to silence them with our first-half performance which sees us both having goals disallowed. Chris finishes off a superb passing move to give us the lead but we lose Stuart Ripley with an injury and it has a disruptive effect on us. It turns out to be a game of two halves with Newcastle grabbing an equaliser through Robert Lee and earning a replay. We are drawn against either Middlesbrough or Swansea at home in the fourth round, so that's a big incentive to win the replay.

After the game, I go straight to Mum and Dad's. They don't live in the same house where I grew up as a lad, having moved into a bungalow a year ago. My early memories as a youngster all revolve around football. I was brought up in a three-bedroomed council house on the sort of football-daft estate where you had a ball thrown at your feet as soon as you could walk. Virtually every day, straight from school, all the kids in the street would be changed and out on to the nearby stretch of wasteland where we played out our football dreams.

Kevin Keegan was always my idol but there was also Chris

Waddle, Peter Beardsley and a young, emerging Paul Gascoigne to feed our fantasies. I used to long for the day when I could pull on the famous black and white striped shirt. It wasn't to be because, although I went to St James's Park for trials, the offer to join Southampton was made when I left school. I felt it would be a better move to build both my career and character and so it proved to be. Dad was a sheet metal worker and, though money was tight, my parents always seemed to find enough cash to provide me with my football gear. I would save all my pocket money as well to get any football paraphernalia I could lay my hands on. I am proud of my upbringing, both on a personal and football level, and I shall be eternally grateful for the sacrifices Mum and Dad made for me.

We have a smashing night and the two grandparents are delighted to spend some time with their new granddaughter Hollie.

TUESDAY 10TH

Back to work after a day off yesterday, and there is a bit of a football bombshell awaiting us after we finish training. The main item on Teletext in the training ground lounge reveals that Andy Cole is joining Manchester United from Newcastle for £6m, with Keith Gillespie moving to St James's Park. It makes the whole deal worth £7m. No one can quite believe it at first. We all knew Manchester United were in the hunt for a new striker but assumed, like everyone else, that Stan Collymore was the main target. For the first time ever Kevin Keegan is under fire from his adoring Newcastle public who cannot believe he has let their goal-machine Cole leave. As usual Keegan handles the situation superbly, explaining to the fans who turn up to remonstrate with him that the deal will benefit Newcastle in the long run. It is hard not to agree with him. He will go out and buy two or three players with the money and I'm sure Newcastle will become a stronger side for it. Cole has had an astonishing run of success but his goals have dried up recently. When a side rely so heavily on one person to score, they can struggle when he goes through barren spells. So it has proved to be with Cole.

Andy is an out-and-out goal-scorer – and a phenomenal one – but maybe Kevin will look for someone who has a greater all-round contribution to make.

Once all the furore dies down, it is clear that both clubs are happy with the deal. United have a striker with a proven record and Newcastle have £6m to spend plus a fine young prospect in Gillespie.

WEDNESDAY 11TH

Another day off but I seem to spend most of it trying to arrange tickets for members of my family for next week's FA Cup replay against Newcastle. We are given five each but I need a dozen and, thankfully, I can rely on the generosity of my colleagues to satisfy my requirements.

FRIDAY 13TH

The gaffer is back at the training ground today looking none the worse for wear after his date with the surgeon. We are pleased to see him, and we suspect he is pleased that life has just gone on as normal at the club without him. We know he has been picking the team during his recovery from his operation but when a club is enjoying a successful run you tend to run on automatic pilot.

There are some very emotional TV pictures tonight showing Paul Merson at his first press conference since he admitted his problems with drink, gambling and cocaine. I know I had a go at him when the revelations were first made but it's hard not to have some sympathy with him now that he is trying to put his life back in order. It must be very harrowing for him to have to appear before the Press and bare his soul but I suppose he has to admit to his addictions before he can overcome them. I don't think I will ever have to face this kind of ordeal. Well, maybe if we win the Championship, I might go out for a drink or four with the lads! I have never been a big drinker. There was a time when I never used to like the taste of alcohol at all but I started to have the odd one or two to be sociable. A couple of lagers or a few glasses of wine are usually my limit.

SATURDAY 14TH

Today's game against Nottingham Forest is a big one for us. We know if we win we can go six points clear at the top because Manchester United are not playing Newcastle until tomorrow. Injuries to Stuart Ripley and Graeme Le Saux and Tim Sherwood's suspension means we have to chop and change but we know we have capable deputies in Alan Wright, Robbie Slater and Ian Pearce, with the versatile Paul Warhurst moving into midfield. The first half is a bit of a stalemate, although Forest have to soak up a lot of pressure from us. In the second half, Warhurst scores, helped by a deflection from Carl Tiler – we are still getting some lucky breaks in front of goal – before Jason Wilcox adds a second. A header from Chris Sutton is helped into the net by Steve Chettle for our third and that starts a debate about whose goal it is. Naturally Chris insists it is his. I doubt whether Chettle wants it but there is a special panel to adjudicate on such matters now, so we will have to await their decision. I could have settled the argument myself because if Chettle had missed the ball I would have put it into the net myself.

Interestingly, Stan Collymore has a very quiet match and you have to wonder whether he has been affected by United's move for Cole, because he was the hot tip to move to Old Trafford for most of the season.

SUNDAY 15TH

Lainya, Chloe, Hollie and I join the Ruddock family for lunch at our favourite Italian restaurant in Formby but we make sure we are back for the Manchester United-Newcastle game on Sky. There's a really explosive atmosphere, though some of the heat is taken out of it through agreement of the two clubs that Cole and Gillespie should not figure in the match. Nevertheless, Keegan has stoked the fires on Tyneside through the sale of his star striker, but all is forgiven as the home fans give him a rapturous reception. Who else but Mark Hughes should give United the lead in the first half? He was linked with a £2m move to Everton in the aftermath of Cole's arrival and his future at Old Trafford has been uncertain ever since it was revealed he has not been offered the extended contract he was seeking. I find that hard to comprehend. Hughes is the key component in the United attack because of his strength and ability to hold the ball and wait for his colleagues to join him. Eric Cantona gets a lot of acclaim – and rightly so – but if you take Hughes away, United are not the same force. Now it looks like they will have to do without him for a considerable time though, because in scoring the opening goal he collides with goalkeeper Pavel Srnicek and is carried off with a gash in his leg and suspected ligament damage. Newcastle stage a mighty recovery and equalise through Paul Kitson, ironically the player who has been given the task of filling Cole's boots. A 1-1 draw is a good result for us because it keeps daylight between ourselves and the chasing pack.

MONDAY 16TH

A look at the Premiership table this morning makes satisfying reading. We are five points ahead of United, with a game in hand and a far superior goal difference, which is virtually worth another point to us. There is a mystifying story in the newspapers today, provided by Forest's Dutch international striker Bryan Roy. According to him, 'Blackburn play to score goals and not to entertain.' Pardon? I always thought the finest form of entertainment was to put the ball in the back of the net as often as possible. A glance at the League table reveals that we have scored more goals than anyone this season. A bit of Double Dutch if you ask me!

WEDNESDAY 18TH

A long soak in the bath at the training ground followed by a couple of hours sleep at the hotel is my preparation for the Newcastle replay. I never have any problem sleeping before a game – only afterwards when every single incident is played over and over again in my mind. My main concern before the kick-off is to get enough tickets for my relatives. I need twenty in the end, mostly for people who have come down from the north-east and, though it proves to be a tall order, I manage to acquire them all. Inside Ewood Park I realise that I have helped to swell the huge contingent of some 6,000 Newcastle fans who have made the trip down for the game and are making a hell of a din in support of their team.

We miss a couple of chances early in the game but the 0-0 score at half-time is probably a fair reflection of the proceedings. Marc Hottiger gives Newcastle the lead with a tremendous strike from 25 yards out and after Chris Sutton levels the scores, I feel pretty certain the replay is heading for extra time. Lee Clark has other ideas, however, and with five minutes left he wins it with a fierce cross-shot which beats Tim Flowers at the near post. Tim receives some criticism for this and to be fair to him, his first words when he comes into the dressing-room are, 'It was my fault.' But you will not find any of his team-mates laying the blame at his door. That's not the way we do things and, in any case, we all appreciate what an outstanding goalkeeper Tim is and how many times he has come to our rescue this season.

There is a huge feeling of disappointment in the dressing-room now that we have been knocked out of our third cup competition of the season. We are left with just the Premiership title to play for. We will settle for that but we know we have to roll up our sleeves and give 110 per cent between now and the end of the season if we are to lay our hands on the biggest prize of them all.

THURSDAY 19TH

It's half-past three in the morning before I get to sleep, the baby wakes us at half-past five and although we have been given a day off, I still have to get up early to fulfil a list of commercial engagements.

First I have to be at the Umbro premises at 10.30 for a photo shoot in the new England kit. Then it's on to Old Trafford at 1.30 to join Rob Jones, Tim Flowers, Paul Parker, Gary Pallister and Terry Venables for a photograph and video session arranged by Green Flag – who are the new sponsors for the national team. Finally, I travel across the Pennines to the Alfred McAlpine Stadium in Huddersfield to take part in a promotion for my mobile phone sponsors, British Telecom, along with the comic Jim Bowen who is an avid Blackburn Rovers supporter. There are 13,000 entry cards from over 100 Telecom branches inside a big football and it is my job to make the prize draw. The first branch to be pulled out three times wins a car and I threaten to finish the whole proceedings in a few minutes flat when Sheffield is the name on both of the first two tickets. Eventually, the draw stretches to 38 names and Lincoln are the lucky winners of the car. The event finishes later than I expected and I stay at a hotel in Huddersfield for the night.

FRIDAY 20TH

It takes me 25 minutes to find my way out of Huddersfield but I still manage to arrive at the training ground in time to be greeted by a posse of pressmen wanting interviews about Sunday's game against Manchester United. The same old questions crop up about me and United and I provide them with the same answers. Training is short and not very sweet for me when Alan Wright accidently catches me on the hip with his knee and I have to limp off for treatment which continues well into the afternoon. If the game was tomorrow I would be struggling to make it but even with the extra 24 hours it is going to be touch and go.

SATURDAY 21ST

I don't train again today because my hip is still very sore but the treatment seems to be working and I am confident of being fit as we travel to Manchester for our overnight stay in a hotel.

SUNDAY 22ND

This is one of the big days of the season. Victory over United can put us seven points clear of them with a game in hand and they know that defeat will leave them with a real mountain to climb. Before the action begins I have to take more stick from my team-mates about a couple of newspaper headlines which claim Newcastle are ready to pay £10m for me. It is all news to me but I can see where the story originates. Newcastle have a vast amount of money to spend from the sale of Andy Cole and I am on record as saying that, at some stage of my career, I would love to play for my hometown team. I think that applies to any footballer who ever supported Newcastle as a lad but it doesn't mean I am ready to dash off to St James's Park, because I am very happy at Blackburn. On this occasion I think the journalists have put two and two together and come up with five, but at least the stories create a bit of fun for the lads and help ease the tension before the match.

You can cut the atmosphere with a knife, however, when we go for our usual pre-match stroll because our hotel is relatively close to Old Trafford and there are several hundred United fans milling around outside. As usual, I am the target for much of their hatred. 'There's only one greedy b*****d' is the popular chant whenever we face United and I assume it is because their supporters still believe I chose to sign for Blackburn due to the money I was offered by Jack Walker. That's absolute nonsense. What they don't know is that I never even had talks with Alex Ferguson because he did not put in a successful bid to Southampton. The only decision left open to me was whether to sign for Blackburn, which I was delighted to do after a day of talks with Kenny Dalglish. The abuse from the United fans is not pleasant but you have to accept it, bite your tongue, walk away and don't give any hint that you are rattled by it.

My hip is still quite sore and I need a pain-killing injection before the kick-off, which does the trick. We are disappointed with our display and, after United dominate the first half, we are lucky still to be level at 0-0. We improve slightly after the break and create a couple of half-chances but it looks as if the game is drifting to a goalless conclusion which suits us, even though we haven't deliberately set out to contain them. Then United snatch the lead with a headed goal by Eric Cantona from Ryan Gigg's superb cross and suddenly we are up against it in a big way. All is not lost – or so we think – and I manage to climb above Roy Keane at the far post and head the ball back across the goal for Tim Sherwood to beat Peter Schmeichel with a fine, brave header. To our amazement the referee, Paul Durkin, disallows it for a push by me on Keane. I cannot believe it. I did raise my arms because that's the only way you can get enough leverage to climb for a high ball, but I barely touched him. The real giveaway is that Roy did not raise a murmur of protest, which confirms my opinion that I did not foul him. I keep my feelings to myself because I don't want to get booked or sent off, but inside I am seething with anger. It hurts even more when I learn in the players' lounge afterwards from someone who knows Keane that he is admitting he was not pushed. For the second time this season against United we feel we have been affected by a refereeing decision (remember the penalty award and Henning Berg's red card at Ewood Park). But we dare not let it affect us and must use it as a form of motivation. After the setback at our place, we closed ranks and became even more determined and difficult to beat. That is what we have to do again. We are still a point ahead of United with a game in hand and there are a few clubs who would gladly swap places with us.

Because Lainya has gone back to Southampton for a few days for her sister's wedding preview, Tim, Mike and I pick up a McDonalds takeaway on the way home only to find, when I drop Mike off, that Mrs Newell has cooked dinner. I go to bed with a full stomach but my emotions drained. I hardly manage a wink of sleep.

MONDAY 23RD

We have been given a couple of days off but because I am still suffering some discomfort from my hip I go to the training ground for an hour of treatment. I return home for a lazy afternoon and go to Tim's house for tea. Jane Flowers is an excellent cook and Tim's a very domesticated husband who does the washing-up and helps to bath the children. I get home and go to bed early for a long uninterrupted sleep.

WEDNESDAY 25TH

Back to a fairly routine day of training and I manage to make it home before a heavy storm leaves a two-inch layer of snow on the ground. I am cooking for myself tonight – another ready-made meal – but I have to ring Lainya first to find out how the cooker works, as well as the washing-machine because we are still waiting for the laundry service to be set up at the training ground. I don't think I am really suited to bachelorhood.

I receive a call from Lainya's brother, Gareth, in the evening to say he has just heard on the radio that Eric Cantona was sent off in United's game against Crystal Palace and attacked a fan as he made his way to the dressing-room. I don't believe him at first or at least think he is exaggerating but, when I see it for myself on the news, I can't believe my own eyes. For a professional footballer to launch such an assault on a member of the public is totally unacceptable. Everyone has always known that Eric has a short fuse but not that he was capable of anything like this. The argument that he was provoked by fans as he made his way around the track doesn't wash. Every player has to live with abusive comments but the golden rule is that you don't get involved. As I mentioned before the United game, their fans can be pretty cruel – not just with remarks directed at me but also at my wife. Although I have often felt like having a go back, it's not worth it. Cantona has let himself down and must prepare himself for the consequences because there is going to be an almighty uproar about his actions. He is a terrifically talented player who has brought immense pleasure to our game, but I am sure that the football authorities will not excuse him for what has happened at Selhurst Park.

THURSDAY 26TH

The Cantona affair is the talk of the training ground today – before, during and after we go out to work. Most of us find it difficult to put our feelings into words, unlike the *Sun* which devotes around ten pages to the incident. News filters through that United have suspended the Frenchman until the end of the season, though really they have no choice. The United board deserves some credit for taking such positive action. In acting so promptly they have done the Football Association's job for them but who is to say there will not be further punishment? There is also speculation that Cantona will walk away from the English game rather than be left kicking his heels for the rest of the campaign. I am sure he realises that in one reckless moment he has severely damaged United's League and FA Cup prospects. Of course, we are aware that it could work to the benefit of Blackburn Rovers but this is not really a time to gloat.

FRIDAY 27TH

Lainya has delayed her return from Southampton until today because there is supposed to be an improvement in the weather. So much for the forecasters. More heavy snow falls and we have to settle for a light-hearted training game in treacherous conditions. There is another downfall after training and it takes me two hours to get home but poor Lainya takes six hours to battle her way through the atrocious weather and traffic.

In the evening I get a phone call from the former England manager Graham Taylor, who is doing a fine job steering Wolves towards the top of the First Division. We chat generally about football and our respective seasons. My respect for him as a man and manager has not wavered despite the unfortunate end to his international career.

SATURDAY 28TH

I have not scored for four games, so this seems a good day to try out the new pair of Umbro boots which have just come on to the market. It takes just three minutes of our match against Ipswich for them to do the trick as I beat Craig Forrest with a powerful shot. I get another goal before half-time with another explosive shot into the top corner. These boots are made for scoring. Tim Sherwood makes it three and when Ipswich pull one back time seems to be running out for me to make it a hat-trick. But with the clock showing 4.45 p.m., Phil Whelan brings me down in the penalty area and I am able to notch my third from the spot. That's my third hat-trick of the season and it gives me as much pleasure as the previous two. There is no greater feeling for me than putting the ball in the net. If I score one I want another. If I am on two goals I want three; a hat-trick, and I'm still going flat out for a fourth. My hunger for goals is never satisfied. I am on a real high after the game but I have a sobering duty to perform. A friend of Jack Hixon's has asked him if a girl from Oxford can come and meet me. She is 27 and suffering from cancer and is apparently terminally ill. She is made very welcome in the players' lounge and is thrilled at the welcome she receives. Things like this bring you back down to earth with a bump.

A few of us join Mike Newell to help him celebrate his 30th birthday at a restaurant called the Bistro French in Preston, where they specialise in sixties and seventies music. Tim Flowers has cried off because he has to go home to see his mother-in-law. Can you believe that?

Bistro French is the sort of place where they actually encourage you to get up on the table to dance and I have to confess I am a little the worse for wear at the end of the evening as I leap into action. But if you cannot celebrate and let your hair down after scoring a hat-trick on your 100th appearance for the club, when can you?

SUNDAY 29TH

I don't often suffer from hangovers but today is an exception. Fresh air is the best cure and Chloe and I go for a long walk in the woods, which does the trick.

TUESDAY 31ST

Torrential rain is falling and training is pretty miserable. Chris Sutton has a day off because he is getting married. The things some people will do to skip training! A few of the lads go to the ceremony and the rest of us attend the party in the evening. Tim is missing again because he wants to prepare for tomorrow's match against Leeds. The gaffer goes to the wedding and then passes the baton on to Ray Harford to keep an eye on us at the evening do. There is a vast amount of water consumed.

FEBRUARY 1995

WEDNESDAY 1ST

What a start to the game against Leeds. I am clean through in the opening minute and John Lukic saves my shot with his legs. They go straight to the other end and Brian Deane is brought down by Tim Flowers, who leaves the referee with no alternative but to send him off. So much for Tim's preparation the night before – all for two minutes of action. It all adds to an explosive atmosphere and the game begins to boil over when we are awarded a penalty for a push on Chris Sutton. Graeme Le Saux and Carlton Parlmer are involved in a bit of a fracas but it is no more than them tossing a couple of handbags at each other. Tempers are still stretched to the limit and Gary McAllister's penalty equaliser earns Leeds a point. The action continues after the final whistle and a Blackburn fan tries to attack the referee, Rodger Gifford. Fortunately our substitute keeper Bobby Mimms manages to prevent him from making any contact, or we could have found ourselves in real trouble. Even so, we have to face an FA inquiry for the incident.

FRIDAY 3RD

I ring Tim after training to wish him a happy 28th birthday but I find him in a depressed mood. A visit to a specialist has confirmed that he broke his toe in the collision with Brian Deane and could be out of action for four weeks. It looks as if the wheel of fortune is turning against us again but there are sure to be many more twists and turns before the destiny of the title is known.

SATURDAY 4TH

On the way down to London for tomorrow's game against Spurs we hear on the radio that Manchester United have beaten Aston Villa 1-0 and have closed the gap on us at the top to two points. We thought that the title race was going to go right to the wire and it is certainly beginning to shape up that way. Andy Cole scored United's winner at Old Trafford – his first goal since his record-busting move – and that is an ominous sign. It will relieve a lot of the pressure on him now that he is off the mark. To be Britain's most expensive player isn't always easy to live with but, to be honest, I thrived on it. I saw it as a privilege to be rated so highly – not that I thought I was worth £3.3m – and it gave me the extra incentive to go out and show I could give real value for money for Blackburn Rovers. Chris Sutton seemed to take it in his stride as well when he joined us for £5m and now the onus is on Andy to show he can live up to his fee.

SUNDAY 5TH

Spurs catch us on an off-day and we find ourselves a couple of goals down with a shot from Jurgen Klinsmann which drills through stand-in keeper Bobby Mimms' legs and one from Darren Anderton which goes into the net off Colin Hendry. The breaks are still not going our way but we pull a goal back when Tim Sherwood lashes the ball home from my head-down. Interestingly, this is almost a replica of the goal that got away against Manchester United. I climb up above Gary Mabbutt and make faint contact with him – just as I did with Roy Keane – but this time no foul is awarded against me. Still, it's too late to start up that old argument. It's also too late for us to get back into this game once Nick Barmby heads Tottenham's third goal. A few arguments develop in the dressing-room afterwards with heated words exchanged about how we might have prevented their goals but it is all heat-of-the-moment stuff and a sign of the frustration we're feeling after picking up just four points out of the twelve.

MONDAY 6TH

Mike Newell and I spend our day off on the Hillside golf course in Southport and the relaxed atmosphere is a pleasant change after the intensity of recent weeks on the football pitch. I win a competitive match on the eighteenth hole and Mike has to buy the bacon and egg sandwiches. I arrive home to discover I am in the England squad for the friendly against the Republic of Ireland – and so is my Blackburn team-mate and skipper Tim Sherwood. His is a thoroughly deserved call-up because of his consistency over the last couple of years. Tim is a competitive player, who passes the ball well, gets from penalty area to penalty area and chips in with his fair portion of goals. What more could you ask for from a midfielder? Nick Barmby and Sol Campbell of Spurs are the surprise inclusions but judging by their performances against us yesterday they are also bang on form.

TUESDAY 7TH

We are expecting a tough training session with lots of running today but the balls are out and it's fairly leisurely. The main item of discussion is the news that Chelsea's Dennis Wise has been convicted of an assault on a taxi driver. As a result he is pulled out of the England squad, though Terry Venables has no alternative. It's another blow for football's battered image and something we could do without. When will all the bad publicity end?

Footballers can be sitting targets for anyone out to cause trouble and we always have to be on our guard. I would not want to shut myself away from the general public because I enjoy meeting fans and chatting to them. But there will always be the odd few who are not satisfied with a brief and friendly exchange of words. I was with Mike Newell once after a match against one of his former clubs, Everton, when we popped into a local pub for a quick drink. An Everton supporter came over and asked Mike, 'Where do your loyalties lie?' We tried to be friendly with him but he kept labouring the point and in the end became abusive. It could have turned nasty but didn't. It was a typical situation where two players wanting to do something normal could have been caught up in a headline-making incident through no fault of their own.

THURSDAY 9TH

Only six members of the first team squad are in for training today with a long queue for the treatment table and Henning Berg away on international duty. But it is good to hear that long-term absentee Kevin Gallacher is in action again and has got through his comeback in the reserves without mishap. Hopefully, David Batty is only another four weeks away from returning and once these two are pushing for first team selection again, it will be like signing a couple of new players in readiness for the title run-in.

SATURDAY 11TH

Sky have chosen our match against Sheffield Wednesday for their live Sunday coverage which means we are powerless to prevent Manchester United from taking over at the top of the Premiership today. They get there in the best possible way for their supporters – a thumping 3-0 away win against their fierce local rivals Manchester City. There is no point in feeling sorry for ourselves about being knocked off the top. Our recent run of results has left a lot to be desired and we have to start winning again – and quickly.

SUNDAY 12TH

Our kick-off time has been put back to five o'clock to avoid clashing with the ITV coverage of the Coca-Cola semi-final between Swindon and Bolton. The television companies seem to exercise a great deal of control over fixtures these days but they plough so many millions of pounds into the game they do have a right to call the tune. I find it difficult to know what to do with myself though, after having a lie-in until around eleven. There are still six hours to go before the game starts and it drags very slowly. When I finally arrive at the ground, there is bad news waiting with Jason Wilcox joining Stuart Ripley and Tim Flowers on the list of injured absentees and Graeme Le Saux mising through suspension. We make a good start, however, and Tim Sherwood puts us in front with a blinding shot from outside the area. Chris Waddle equalises but Mark Atkins restores our lead and we are well in control. Another controversial sending off occurs when the Wednesday goalkeeper, Kevin Pressman, is given a red card for deliberately handling the ball outside the area. The Sheffield players argue that the shot from Paul Warhurst was going wide and, in any case, Des Walker was covering the effort on the goal-line. Their complaints are to no avail and Pressman has to go. Chris Woods performs well as his replacement but I manage to head in a third goal in worsening weather conditions. If the torrential rain had started half an hour earlier, we might have struggled to finish the full 90 minutes, but we end up worthy winners and are back on top of the Premiership.

There is not much time for Tim Sherwood, Graeme Le Saux and I to celebrate because there is a car waiting to whisk us away to Blackpool airport. There we board a private jet to Heathrow and link up with the rest of the England squad for Wednesday's International in Dublin.

MONDAY 13TH

Apart from the warm-up, Tim Sherwood and I are excused training today because we played a full game yesterday. Our only activity is to join in a mass signing session of balls, tops, etc.

TUESDAY 14TH

The England team is announced after training and Matthew Le Tissier's selection to partner me up-front in a 4-4-2 formation attracts the most attention. The Press are waiting for us at Luton airport and several of them want to talk to me about Matty. I make a jokey remark about how glad I was to leave Southampton and join Blackburn because I was fed up of doing all his running for him. They all take it in the right spirit – except one, who treats it as a serious comment about my former team-mate.

It doesn't worry me too much but I wish some reporters would try and be a bit more accurate. There are quite a few Irish fans waiting for us at Dublin airport. Dublin's a place I love to visit. The people are always very friendly and seem genuinely pleased to see us.

WEDNESDAY 15TH

On the radio we learn that there have been a few disturbances around the city involving England fans. It is something we have come to expect on away trips and so we do not pay much attention to it. There is a 6.15 p.m. kick-off and we are at the ground early for a stroll on the pitch. Lansdowne Road is essentially a rugby stadium and the playing area reflects this with its long grass and bobbly surface. I bump into the groundsman, Graham Scurr, who used to look after The Dell when I was at Southampton, and he confirms that the pitch needs less care and attention because it is mainly used for rugby.

As the kick-off time approaches, there is little evidence of trouble brewing among the fans. The booing during the playing of both national anthems is unfortunate but, sadly, that is also fairly commonplace these days. My attention is focused fully on the start of the game and I am not at all distracted by what is happening off the pitch. When the Irish go 1-0 up through David Kelly, the first signs of disturbance emerge. A section of English fans seems to be hurling objects at those below them in a lower deck of the stadium but I still think it is an over-reaction when the referee takes the players off the field.

Back in the dressing-room we are still not fully aware of how serious the trouble is. Terry Venables uses the time positively to try to change the way we are playing. Soon, it is clear that the outbreak of violence is serious. Here we go again. I thought we had got rid of this curse from our game years ago. Now it's obvious we have become too complacent about it. A lot of the crowd control is left in the hands of stewards these days and though they do a good job they do not carry the same power and authority as the police. It obviously hasn't taken the louts long to realise that they can take advantage of the relaxation in security.

I venture into the corridor outside the dressing-room and bump into Umbro's Martin Prothero. I am chatting to him when a little Irish lad of no more than eight years old is brought in by First Aid men. He sees me and blurts out, 'I f*****g hate you.' We think he is suffering from shock but, when Martin asks him if he is badly hurt, he doesn't want to know. 'I am a Manchester United fan,' he snaps. His mother is just a few feet away and she doesn't say a word to reprimand him. What chance have we got when kids are allowed to behave like this?

The match is eventually abandoned and we cannot wait to get home. Unfortunately we are on a scheduled flight which is not due to depart from Dublin until ten o'clock so we have a lengthy wait. I want to telephone Lainya from the airport but the phone has been smashed. The wrong kind of English fans have beaten me to it. There is a massive media presence at Luton when we arrive back but we are all careful not to make too many comments because we are still not fully aware of the extent of the problem.

THURSDAY 16TH

The television and newspaper pictures this morning leave everyone in no doubt that the eruption of hooliganism is far more serious than we believed. It is difficult to take it all in but I suppose there have been indications recently that trouble has been brewing. First there was the recent attempt by a Blackburn fan to attack referee Rodger Gifford. The club have been cleared of any blame for that by the FA but it was an ominous incident. There was also trouble at the Manchester City-Manchester United derby game and many people believe the Eric Cantona affair at Crystal Palace did not help the situation. The infuriating thing is that the troublemakers in Dublin are not real football fans. They are there for their own perverse political reasons and care nothing for the national team or the game as a whole.

I spend most of the day reflecting on the events of yesterday.

I do not believe the match should have been abandoned. In doing so, the authorities have handed victory to the louts. I would have preferred to see the stadium cleared and, if necessary, the match completed behind locked doors.

FRIDAY 17TH

We are back in training and most of the lads have enjoyed four days off. It is a pity I couldn't have enjoyed the break with them. We finish with a hard session of keep-ball – an exercise where one team has to try and dispossess the other in one half of the pitch. My team hardly gets a kick. Suddenly we realise we are playing seven men against nine. Ray Harford picked the sides and gets some awful stick!

SATURDAY 18TH

No game this weekend because we are out of the FA Cup and no League fixture has been arranged. As expected, we are put through a very vigorous running session, while Chris Sutton and I volunteer for an extra half-hour with Tony Parkes to work on our finishing. It doesn't matter how regularly the goals are flowing, you can never spend too much time sharpening your shooting in and around the box. In the evening Lainya and I, Tim and Jane Flowers and Mike and Catherine Newell reward ourselves for an active day's work by going out for a Chinese meal.

SUNDAY 19TH

The most energetic thing I do today is take the dog out for a long walk with Lainya and the kids. After that I don't move from in front of the television set where I watch the FA Cup ties between Newcastle and Manchester City and Manchester United and Leeds. I would much rather still be playing in the Cup but at least this weekend has given the whole of our squad a little breather and time to recharge our batteries in readiness for the title challenge ahead. It also gives us a chance to let any little bumps and bruises heal, which is not always possible when you are playing three games in a week.

MONDAY 20TH

We all get a lift from seeing David Batty back in full training today. If he is match fit for the Championship finale after his long lay-off, it really will be like signing a £5m player.

WEDNESDAY 22ND

Tonight's match against Wimbledon at Ewood Park is our first competitive action for ten days – and it shows. We get a bright enough start and I score with a header before Mark Atkins makes it 2-0. But Efan Ekoku pulls one back and Wimbledon make us work hard after the break when we look pretty sluggish. The playing surface is a real mudbath again. It's probably the worst surface I have ever played on and yet it used to be one of the best in the country. The non-stop rain and number of matches we have played are taking their toll and unless there is a dramatic improvement in the weather, our form could be affected if we are not careful. We are a team who like to play the ball up to the strikers quickly but that does not make us a route one outfit. We do have players who like to pass and run with the ball and that isn't easy when you're playing on a glue-pot pitch. I feel sure the conditions have contributed to some of our indifferent performances at home recently.

Mike Newell makes his first starting appearance of the season as replacement for the suspended Chris Sutton and he works hard and plays his part in the victory. But, given the choice, he would have picked a more inviting fixture for his comeback. 'I've waited nine months for a full game in the first team and it's just my luck that it's against Wimbledon on a pitch like that,' he groans afterwards.

THURSDAY 23RD

I have to have treatment on a leg injury instead of training but it is nothing too serious. I visit the Umbro headquarters in the afternoon to make a presentation of one of my signed England shirts to one of their staff – an avid Blackburn fan – who is retiring after twenty years.

FRIDAY 24TH

Eric Cantona is dealt with by the Football Association today for the incident with the fan at Crystal Palace and his suspension is extended until the end of September with an additional £10,000 fine. I think even he will agree that he is lucky to get off so lightly. There is a lot of speculation about whether he will see out his ban and still be a United player when it is over. I think he will because he seems particularly happy at Old Trafford and I think it unlikely that he will let down the good name of his club again.

It has been another bad week for football with George Graham being sacked by Arsenal for allegedly taking a 'bung' from the transfer fee which took John Jensen from Brondby to Highbury. If Graham did that he deserves the punishment. I only wish the game could receive some favourable publicity once in a while. Spectator interest is high and so is the quality of the football, but all the good things are being overshadowed by the bad.

SATURDAY 25TH

The *Sun* is carrying another 'exclusive' story about me today. Apparently, Umbro have agreed to pay me £2m to wear their boots for the rest of my playing days. In truth, there have been some preliminary discussions with the firm but no agreement has been reached and no figures finalised.

Back to reality and the visit of Norwich City to Ewood Park. They beat us at Carrow Road and will be looking to complete a double, especially as they need points to climb away from the danger zone. Even though we are still without the suspended Chris Sutton, there is good news on the selection form with Tim Flowers, Graeme Le Saux, Stuart Ripley and Jason Wilcox all fit again after injury. The bad news is that our pitch has gone from one extreme to another. The mudbath has turned into a desert – a dry, bumpy surface which makes passing the ball virtually impossible.

Even allowing for the conditions, we don't play very well and

Norwich keep us at bay without too many problems. We miss a couple of half-chances but as we are chasing a winner towards the end, we leave ourselves unguarded at the back and Tim Flowers has to show why we regard him as the country's number one goalkeeper with two outstanding saves.

We are very disappointed at the goalless outcome but there is a better score awaiting us in the dressing-room after the final whistle. We don't hear it until we come out of the bath because the kick-off between Everton and Manchester United had been delayed by traffic congestion. The Merseysiders' 1-0 victory is greeted euphorically by Blackburn players and fans alike. Once it has sunk in, there are tinges of regret because we have missed the opportunity to open the gap even wider.

We are still three points clear of United with a superior goal difference but no one is pretending it is a two-horse race because Newcastle are creeping up behind both of us. Their 3-1 win over Aston Villa maintains an impressive run of results and striker Paul Kitson deserves credit for stepping into Andy Cole's scoring boots and, of course, so does Kevin Keegan for sticking his neck out and making the biggest transfer gamble of the season. They are now twelve points behind us and nine behind United with a game in hand – if that seems a tall order, don't forget we were sixteen points adrift last season and twice squandered the chance to take over the leadership.

Make no mistake, we are all looking over our shoulders at Newcastle. It is becoming a title race to remember and it has certainly captured the attention of everyone in Blackburn. Everywhere you go people seem to be talking of little else and it is amazing how the expectations of our supporters have risen from the days when the club was struggling in the old Second and Third Divisions.

There isn't a more enthusiastic fan than Jack Walker, who flies over without fail from his home in Jersey for every game, both at home and away. He is in the dressing-room before and after the match, shaking the hand of each player and wishing him well. It is always a delight to see him.

In the evening Lainya and I join Neil and Sarah Ruddock for a meal at a favourite fish restaurant of ours in Southport. I choose mussels and oysters – my first encounter with seafood since my horrible experience in Portugal in the summer – but the chef puts his hand on his heart and insists they are fresh and well cooked.

SUNDAY 26TH

Lainya's mum and dad are with us for the weekend and we all spend a day in the fresh air at the Martin Mere Wildfowl Trust where Chloe is in her element feeding the ducks and geese. In the evening we dine out again in the company of Oldham's Ian Snodin, whose wife is celebrating her birthday, and Mike Newell and Kevin Sheedy with their respective spouses.

MONDAY 27TH

A routine training session is followed by more exercise with a family visit to our local health club. Lainya works out in the gymnasium because she wants to get her weight down in time for the summer and Chloe and I have a splashing time in the swimming pool. When we get back home I catch the end of Sky TV's review of the season so far and hear Andy Gray tipping Blackburn to win the title on goal difference. I don't think my nerves can stand the strain of such a tight finish.

TUESDAY 28TH

No midweek game so we are given a day off which Mike Newell and I spend on the golf course at Formby. He has his revenge this time, beating me by two holes, and I have to pay the green fees. David Batty gets through his first game for ten months against Rotherham reserves with flying colours. His has an unusual injury – a split bone in his foot – but he has been very patient and hopefully his reward will come with a return to the first team soon. Newcastle beat Ipswich 2-0 at Portman Road and we can really feel their breath on the back of our necks now.

MARCH 1995

WEDNESDAY 1ST

A heavy snowfall cuts our training session short and we all rush in out of the freezing cold into a welcome hot bath. Lainya has a night out at a fashion show and, after I've settled the kids down, I spend another evening in front of the TV watching the FA Cup replay between Southampton and Spurs. I still have a soft spot for my old club and would love to see them have a long run in the competition but after building up a 2-0 lead, it all goes dreadfully wrong and they lose 6-2 after extra time. The one consolation for me is that I have won £10 from Tim Flowers in bets we made on the outcome of this game and Crystal Palace's replay win over Watford.

FRIDAY 3RD

Just when we thought there could not be any more bad publicity for football, there is another so-called 'sleaze' story in the newspapers today. Crystal Palace striker Chris Armstrong is reported to have failed a random drug test because traces of cannabis were found in his system. This of course provides the tabloids with further ammunition to sling at the game. Admittedly, it is more negative news we could have done without, but let's not forget that the vast majority of players and officials have never stepped out of line – but they do not make the headlines.

From a personal point of view, I have never even seen any of these supposed social drugs. I was brought up in an environment where they did not exist. I know some people might look upon me as a goody-goody but I don't go out of my way to cultivate such an image. I like a drink and a good laugh, the same as most players, but I stick to my limits. There is so much media attention on celebrities these days that it only takes one drink too many and a minor indiscretion to find yourself splashed all over the papers. My golden rule is 'be sensible' and if that sounds boring then I would rather be considered that than let myself, my family, my club and my profession down.

SATURDAY 4TH

A mid-moring inspection is required at Villa Park before our game against Aston Villa is given the go-ahead but the pitch is in good condition, considering the heavy snowfalls this week. We get off to a flying start with Colin Hendry scoring with a header from Jason Wilcox's corner. It proves to be the only goal of a game in which we are able to show the value of hard work. It is not a vintage performance as far as the quality of our football is concerned, but we prove that there are few teams in such good physical condition as we are. Nor are many players as willing as us to put the team's cause ahead of individual glory.

It is a superb collective effort, but one player catches my eye today – defender Ian Pearce. He has been one of our unsung heroes in recent weeks and he is particularly outstanding against Villa. He has probably saved the manager a £3m or £4m dip into the transfer market with his displays in the centre of the back four. It is not until the final phase of the game that Villa cause us any problems and they have a loud appeal for a penalty turned down when Colin Hendry stops a shot from Paul McGrath with his hand. The referee is Rodger Gifford, who gave Leeds their late spot-kick against us, and there is a huge sigh of relief when he waves aside Villa's protests. From where I was positioned, Colin threw himself into the tackle and the ball struck his hand, leaving him with no chance of avoiding it. The ref gives us the benefit of the doubt, thankfully.

I finish the match in a fair bit of discomfort. Midway through the second half I clash knees with Gary Charles and I suspect there are a few days' treatment in store for me. As we leave the pitch Ray Harford tells us Manchester United have beaten Ipswich 9-0. They have wiped out our goal difference advantage in one swoop but I rather like the comment of Kenny Dalglish afterwards: 'You only get three points whether you win 9-0 or 1-0.'

On returning home I discover I am not the only casualty in the Shearer household. Chloe has been to the Newells' house and damaged her arm in a fall when she jumped off the settee. It has been put in a sling but fortunately nothing is broken.

SUNDAY 5TH

Just as I thought, my knee is swollen and bruised and I have to visit the training ground for treatment. Already I know it is going to be touch and go whether I am fit for Wednesday's game against Arsenal.

MONDAY 6TH

Another morning in the medical room.

TUESDAY 7TH

After more treatment I travel to Manchester to see the Orthopaedic specialist, Mr Hodgkinson, who assures me that there is no cartilage or ligament damage. That's very heartening and he insists that, once the swelling has gone down, I should be fit for action. Tonight I sit and listen to commentary of the Manchester United-Wimbledon game on the radio – or at least 75 minutes of it. The scores are still level at 0-0 but I cannot stand the suspense and, with fifteen minutes left, I go and have a bath. I emerge to discover United have won 1-0 with a very late goal from Steve Bruce which puts them on top of the table on goal difference. That hurts, but we can reclaim the leadership in 24 hours.

WEDNESDAY 8TH

Back to the treatment table and, although the knee has improved, I still cannot be sure whether I will be fit to face Arsenal.

It is decided to leave it until as late as possible and I arrive at the ground at 5.30 p.m. for a final test. The doctor suggests I have a pain-killing jab and assures me that there is no risk of any medium- or long-term damage. I accept his advice reluctantly because I am always apprehensive about this type of injection, but all my worries are wiped away when we build up a 3-0 lead. I score after four minutes, Graeme Le Saux grabs a second and I convert my tenth penalty of the season – not bad when you consider I missed the first on the opening day against Southampton. It should be a stroll for us for the remainder of the game but the Gunners make a fight of it and Tim Flowers is kept so busy he produces enough top quality saves to earn the Man of the Match award. It is his first of the season and he is given a crate of lager. He refuses to share it with anyone so I suspect he is going to frame it.

We all check into the hotel for the night, content to be back on top. I feel surprisingly pain-free. The injection has worked well.

FRIDAY 10TH

I still require treatment before we travel to Coventry, though the knee is improving all the time. The lads are in high spirits when we sit down for our evening meal and coach driver Paul Stone is the target for a prank. We are all balancing teaspoons on the ends of our noses and when Paul is asked to have a go he is given one which has been held in the flame of a candle. He burns his nose, cries out in pain and everyone falls about in fits of laughter. How childish. It's amazing what sixteen grown men will find to do to amuse themselves when they are away from home!

We have lost one of our first team squad members today. Alan Wright has joined Aston Villa in a £900,000 transfer, which is a great move for him. We will miss having him around the club. He's a good little player, who has been unfortunate because Graeme Le Saux's consistency has stopped him from claiming a regular first team place.

SATURDAY 11TH

We know Coventry are going to be difficult opponents today because they are on a high following Ron Atkinson's appointment as manager a few weeks ago. But we don't realise how much of a task we will be facing. They go ahead deservedly through Dion Dublin and although we have a couple of half-chances and I have a shot cleared off the line, it is probably our worst 45 minutes of the season. In case we do not realise it, the manager and Ray Harford let us know in no uncertain terms at half-time that our performance is unacceptable – though not so politely! There is a lot of shouting and swearing and for the first time this season we are given a thorough rollocking. The effect is remarkable. We spend virtually the whole of the second half camped in Coventry's penalty area, though we have to wait until the closing minutes before equalising. I climb higher than Jonathan Gould to reach Graeme Le Saux's cross and manage to head the ball into the net. I make contact with the Coventry goalkeeper – not deliberately but, as I have said before, it is impossible to jump for a high centre without using your arms for leverage. Even so, some referees would have disallowed it, but Terry Holbrook, whom I have always found to be one of the better officials, sees nothing wrong with it. It gives us a vital point and I make the comment afterwards that it might just be the goal which wins us the Championship. We are four points clear and will remain so over the weekend because Manchester United are playing in the FA Cup tomorrow against QPR.

SUNDAY 12TH

No day of rest for me. More treatment on my knee, which is responding well, but there is still fluid around the joint. In the afternoon I join Mike Newell at Goodison Park to watch the FA Cup game between Everton and Newcastle. Our seats are right in the middle of a group of Geordie fans, who obviously believe the newspaper headlines of a few weeks ago. Some of them even suggest a deal has already been done and that I will be a Newcastle player next season. I smile and reply, 'You know more about this than I do.' I share the disappointment of the Toon Army as Newcastle are knocked out by a Dave Watson goal.

MONDAY 13TH

Still no training for me and there is some quite distressing news when we discover that Jason Wilcox needs surgery to repair a damaged cruciate ligament in his knee and will not play again this season. It has been decided by the management to keep it out of the Press – to leave our opponents in the dark about our future selection plans. The injury is the same one which kept me out for what seemed like an eternity. Jason can rest assured he will be in good hands because his operation is being performed by Mr Dandy, the specialist who did such a fine job on my knee.

There is more gloom and doom on a radio news bulletin as I drive to Manchester airport to catch a flight to London. I hear that Dennis Wise has been given a three-month prison sentence for assaulting a taxi driver and, although he is allowed out on bail pending an appeal, it is another stain on football's image. I wonder if he has been made an example of by the court because of the endless bad publicity.

I visit the Umbro offices in the capital for a photo shoot for a billboard advertisement. It shows me with a big burly Sunday footballer and the caption 'You don't have to be a professional to wear Umbro.' The session seems to take ages to complete and it's very late when I arrive home.

TUESDAY 14TH

No work today with a day at Cheltenham planned for all the players. I rang my jockey mate Brendan Powell yesterday to see if he had any inside knowledge and, although he was unable to provide any racing certainties, he does join us for a drink and a chat in our private box. I am not a great gambler but manage to show a slight profit at the end of the afternoon.

On the coach, we are all stunned to hear the latest bombshell to hit football. Bruce Grobbelaar, John Fashanu and Hans Segers are among five people arrested in connection with police investigations into bribery allegations. This is probably the most difficult of all the recent scandals to accept because it strikes at the very heart of the sport. What confidence can the public have in football if they suspect some of the matches have been fixed? However, nothing has been proved yet.

WEDNESDAY 15TH

Everyone else has a day off to recover from their hangovers but I am back in for more treatment. I don't intend to miss any League games this season because I am the only member of the squad with a 100 per cent appearance record, so I am sticking rigidly to my prescribed treatment. My former Southampton team-mate Jeff Kenna is signing for Blackburn for £1.4m and he will be a very valuable addition. He can play in either full back position or in midfield, so will add significantly to the overall strength of the squad.

I cannot stand the thought of listening to Manchester United's game against Spurs on the radio so I content myself with flicking on the Teletext scores at regular intervals. It is a good result for us – a goalless draw – which underlines how important my equaliser and the point we achieved at Coventry were last Saturday.

THURSDAY 16TH

I manage to train today for the first time in almost two weeks, though nothing too strenuous. I restrict myself to an hour's workout with the goalkeepers. I won't have lost any overall fitness because at this stage of the season, with games coming one after the other, there is enough physical activity to keep the body in good shape. I remember to ring my mate Neil Ruddock to tell him he owes me a favour and that I will accept nothing less than a Liverpool victory over Manchester United on Sunday as payment.

SUNDAY 18TH

The newspapers draw attention to the fact that I need just one more goal against Chelsea today to complete 100 in League football. Only 23 came from 105 full appearances for Southampton but since my move to Blackburn I have netted 76 in 88 full games and six as substitute. I don't feel any greater pressure going into this match. Three points have to be the priority – not personal glory.

We make a terrible start and Mark Stein puts Chelsea in front after three minutes – but it isn't long before I have the chance to reach my ton. Graeme Le Saux, who has been pushed forward into the left of midfield to allow Jeff Kenna to make his debut at full back, hits a long pass through to me and I am left one-on-one with goalkeeper Kevin Hitchcock. These might look like easy chances but sometimes they are the most difficult. Hitchcock stands up and does not allow me much of a target to aim at. He leaves a slightly bigger gap to his right side and is urging me to shoot into that corner. It becomes a battle of wits and I decide to go for full power, high into the goal. As he dives to his right, the ball crashes into the roof of the net. All this happens in a split second and I suppose most of it is instinctive. Goalkeepers are so cunning these days, it always feels good to get one over on them. It also feels great to join the 100 club!

I still remember my first with just as much clarity as the one which has taken me to three figures. I was making my debut as a seventeen year old for Southampton against Arsenal and was as nervous as a kitten until I hit the target. I beat Michael Thomas to a cross from Colin Clarke from the right and my header squeezed through John Lukic's legs. The excitement I felt was overpowering and it inspired me to go on and complete my hat-trick.

Now here I am 97 goals later at a memorable milestone. I learn after today's game that I have become the first player to score 30 goals in the top division in two successive seasons since Jimmy Greaves completed the feat in 1964. It is a privilege to be mentioned in the same breath as him – but enough of individual achievement – there is still a match to be won. We take the lead through Tim Sherwood who chooses to chip the ball over Hitchcock when he is through with only the keeper to beat.

We have sufficient chances to be five or six goals up at half-time but good goalkeeping and poor finishing restrict our victory to 2-1. That's enough to build our lead over United to six points and the celebratory bottle of wine I enjoy with Lainya when I arrive home tastes particularly good.

SUNDAY 19TH

I travel to Birmingham early today for a photo session for a book which is coming out later this year, aimed at giving tips to youngsters on how to score goals. The pictures are being taken at a sports ground near to Tony Stephen's home and before too long we attract the attention of some schoolboys who are training on an adjoining pitch. We manage to bribe them into disappearing with some autographed pictures and a group photograph which we promise to send to them when it is developed. Despite a couple of further interruptions while we shelter from hailstones, the session goes smoothly and quickly.

After lunch at Tony's I watch some of the Sampdoria-AC Milan game on television and am surprised at how deep David Platt is playing in midfield. It does not stop my England team-mate from making his penetrating runs into the opposition penalty area though.

I leave for home and start to listen to the Liverpool-United match on my car radio. I cannot stand it for too long and keep switching over to Radio One. I get very worked up listening to the radio broadcast because whenever the ball gets near the Liverpool area, there is so much excitement in the commentator's voice, that I think a United goal is inevitable. The game is still in progress when I arrive back home and I cannot bear to watch the last ten minutes on TV either. But Lainya soon puts me out of my misery and tells me that Liverpool have won 2-0.

Within 25 minutes of the final whistle, Neil Ruddock is on the telephone asking, 'Was that good enough for you?' I thank him and tell him he can have a bottle of champagne on me later when he attends Ian Rush's testimonial dinner. The League table looks really healthy for us again – six points clear and two goals better than United on goal difference. But let's not get too carried away. There's still a hell of a way to go.

My telephone rings at quarter to four in the morning and even before I answer it, I know who it is. Mr Ruddock is slightly the worse for wear and wants to inform me he has had more than one bottle of champagne. He thinks it must have been about four. I promise him I'll pay for the lot if we win the title.

MONDAY 20TH

After a light training session, I visit the local hospital for a scan on my knee which is still proving to be a little bit niggly. I don't feel any pain during matches, nor immediately afterwards, but I can still sense something slight unusual.

After the scan I have to hurry to Manchester airport to catch a flight to London where I am making an appearance on the BT stand at the Ideal Home Exhibition. The scan results are playing on my mind and although I have arranged to ring the physio Steve Foster for the outcome this evening, I am disappointed to find out he is not at home.

TUESDAY 21ST

Steve rings me on my car phone on my way to the training ground. 'I had better let the doctor explain what is wrong,' he says. My heart sinks. I immediated fear that something serious is wrong. 'Give me the bad news,' I say to Dr Burke. He puts me at ease straight away. Apparently, there is a slight dent at the top of my femur, behind the kneecap. 'It's nothing too serious,' insists the doc. 'It will disappear itself, given a suitable period of rest.'

It is agreed this morning by myself, the doctor and the manager that it is best if I pull out of the England squad for next week's friendly International against Uruguay. I hate to miss out on playing for my country, but I accept the advice that it is best to miss one game now rather than risk being ruled out of the three Internationals in a tournament scheduled for the end of the season. I ring Terry Venables to tell him the decision and he is very understanding.

Incidentally, there is a story in the *Today* newspaper claiming that Inter Milan are going to bid £8m for me and that I have indicated I want to move to Italy at the end of the season, rather than wait until my contract expires in a year's time. Surely this cannot be right. I haven't started my Italian lessons yet!

WEDNESDAY 22ND

A day off but there is a friendly tonight against Accrington Stanley as part of their centenary celebrations. I sit this one out but a crowd of about 6,000 turns out to see us win 2-0. It is a valuable fitness exercise for David Batty and Kevin Gallacher, who joins Chris Sutton on the scoresheet.

THURSDAY 23RD

Bill Thornton of the *Daily Star* rings Tony Stephens to ask him about the latest Inter Milan rumours. Tony insists that, as far as he is concerned, there is no truth in them and the paper carries a story saying, 'Shearer snubs Italian giants.' Sometimes you just cannot win.

It is transfer deadline day today and there are no massive deals. Blackburn sign the Dutch midfielder Richard Witschge on loan for the rest of the season. I cannot remember too much about him but I think I may have played against him or his brother Rob in an international game.

The television and radio news bulletins are crammed with news of Eric Cantona's court case today. He has pleaded guilty to assaulting the Crystal Palace fan and is sent to jail for fourteen days. He is let out on bail pending an appeal and once more football itself is on trial. I view the Cantona case from two angles. If you compare what he did with Dennis Wise's case he has got off rather lightly. But I still cannot help but feel that this has become open season for hammering the game and its professionals and they are being punished more severely than ordinary members of the public.

FRIDAY 24TH

The boss has given me a few days off so I fly to Southampton with Lainya and the kids to spend a few days at her parents' home.

SATURDAY 25TH

Chloe and I go shopping and she selects a nice bunch of flowers for her mum because it's Mother's Day tomorrow. We settle down for a peaceful afternoon when suddenly the phone starts ringing . . . again . . . and again . . . and again. I get at least half a dozen calls from family and friends asking whether I have seen Gary Lineker on the BBC's *Football Focus*. I haven't, but I am told that Gary has been discussing my absence from the England squad, saying, 'I do hope it is a genuine injury.' There was apparently an inference in his comments that I could be faking it in order to save myself for Blackburn's Championship run-in. All the people who ring me are furious at the suggestion. Mike Newell is one of them. He is really angry because he knows the trouble I have been having with my knee. Most of the callers are far more upset about the remarks than I am. Even so, I am disappointed because I have always got on well with Gary and I would have thought he knows me well enough to understand I would never do anything as devious as this. I am immensely proud of playing for my country and would never deliberately miss an International unless I was genuinely injured.

What concerns me slightly is that, because of the public respect Gary commands, it might have planted a seed of doubt in some people's minds and a few might just believe him. I try to put the episode out of my mind and enjoy my evening. Lainya, her sister and her mum go out for the night with some friends, so her dad invites some pals round for a game of cards and a few drinks.

SUNDAY 26TH

I leave the family gathering to travel to Wembley to help launch the new England kit. The Football Association sends a car to pick me up from Southampton with the message, 'Tell Mr Shearer not to forget his boots.' Well, my boots are back at the training ground so I expect to be posing for pictures in my bare feet. Umbro's Simon Marsh is one step ahead of the game, as usual, and there is a pair waiting for me at Wembley.

My diary of commercial activities has been pretty busy recently and I must admit I do enjoy making personal appearances and promoting products. If they started becoming too much of a distraction and affected my football however, I would knock them on the head immediately. I don't think Tony Stephens would allow it to get to that stage, though. Tony has a vast amount of experience, having handled David Platt's business projects for six years, so I trust his judgement.

Tim Flowers and I are chosen to model the new strip and I am impressed with the clean, uncluttered design of the shirts. But I am not so sure about the goalkeeper's outfit. It is bright yellow blended with an odd mixture of other vivid colours. Tim looks like a canary who has been in an explosion in a paint factory. You need sunglasses on to look at him. After the session I fly back to Manchester and as I arrive home Sarah Ruddock, who has been on dog-sitting duty, is just leaving. She looks a little pale and flustered and explains that Candy has caused a bit of a mess in the utility room but she has cleaned it up for me. That's what friends are for!

The local pizza shop provides a welcome evening meal for myself and Lainya's dad who has come back with me to mend some of my garden fencing which has blown down in the storms.

MONDAY 27TH

My break is over and it's back to work, though I still don't join in with the rest of the lads because I have to avoid any physical contact in case my knee flares up again. I restrict my exercise to some weights and step-ups. The manager has a word with me after training about Gary Lineker's remarks. He has rung the BBC on behalf of the club and demanded an apology. The medical report and the scans are available for all to see, though

I don't see why we should have to go out of our way to prove anything to anyone.

TUESDAY 28TH

I train on my own again but the knee is starting to feel much better.

In the afternoon I receive a telephone call from Gary Lineker. He is now aware of my views and is full of apologies. He claims that he was put on the spot on live television and didn't quite mean the words to come out the way they did. He says he will try to put it right in the programme on Saturday.

WEDNESDAY 29TH

After training I travel south to watch England's friendly against Uruguay at Wembley. I meet Tony at a service station on the M6 and we proceed to the Wembley Hilton where an interview has been arranged with an Italian journalist for the big-selling daily newspaper *La Gazzetta dello Sport.* There has been some inevitable speculation about me over there and it is time to put the record straight. Thankfully the interview is conducted in English because my Italian still needs brushing up! Most of the conversation is about my career in England but, sure enough, he asks me whether I will be playing in Italy one day. I give the standard reply: 'I have never even thought about it – I'll cross that bridge when I come to it.' I must get a tape-recording made of that answer because I am sure the question will crop up again and again and again.

I also attend a pre-match function with Trevor Brooking and Gordon Banks where we are asked to discuss England's prospects. Later we have trouble locating our match tickets but, as Tony used to be the sales and marketing director of Wembley Stadium, he manages to use his contacts to get us through the back corridors into our seats.

I sit next to my old boss Lawrie McMenemy and we spend a fair bit of time chatting about the old days at Southampton. I am grateful for his company because the match is a pretty tedious affair, especially in the first half. Uruguay have come for one thing – to defend and frustrate the England team and they certainly achieve that. The crowd gets restless and I think they are unfair on John Barnes who always seems to bear the brunt of any criticism that's flying around.

After the match I complete my duties for the day by presenting the Green Flag Man of the Match award to Darren Anderton. It has been a busy day for me – I think I've had more to do than if I'd been playing in the match. Paul Stone drives Tim Flowers, Neil Ruddock and me up to the M6 service station to collect my car. Nearer home we stop off for a big breakfast at two in the morning. I think I deserve it because I have worked hard – certainly a lot harder than Tim did during the match!

THURSDAY 30TH

The knee is slowly feeling better and I join in my first full training session for several weeks without any discomfort. Afterwards Lex Rover kindly deliver my new sponsored car which they provide in exchange for me undertaking personal appearances for them as well as providing occasional match tickets for their employees and guests.

The first car I had from them had my name emblazoned along the side which I was not too keen on because it attracted attention wherever I went. It got to the point where I was starting to become unhappy about using it, so I was grateful when Lex Rover agreed to remove the markings.

I drive the new car to the airport to pick up Lainya and the girls and it is good to have them back home. The staff at the pizza shop down the road can have a well-deserved rest.

FRIDAY 31ST

Eric Cantona's appeal against his prison sentence is heard today and no one is too surprised when his two weeks in jail are overturned and he is given 120 hours of community service. That seems a much more sensible punishment because prison is far too harsh for a crime of that type.

I still feel that the Manchester United player was being made a scapegoat for football's endless problems, as was Dennis Wise. The big question still remains unanswered, however – will Cantona stay or will he go? Inter Milan have declared their interest in signing him and you have to wonder about the pressure he will face in this country if and when he eventually makes his comeback. He creates a stir after his court appearance when he addresses a press conference and talks about seagulls following trawlers because they think sardines will be thrown into the sea . . . No one is quite sure what he is on about but I reckon it is his obscure way of having a go at the media for hounding him over the last few weeks.

The Blackburn squad check into a hotel in St Helens tonight in preparation for tomorrow's match at Everton and we watch the Sky TV football preview which carries an item on the PFA Player of the Year awards. I consider it a privilege to be one of the six nominees for the main award along with Matthew Le Tissier, Eric Cantona, Paul Ince, Jurgen Klinsmann and my club-mate Tim Sherwood. We have to wait for the awards dinner on Sunday week to discover who the winner is.

APRIL 1995

SATURDAY 1ST

Gary Lineker keeps his promise on *Football Focus* and tells the nation that the knee injury which kept me out of the England game has been a problem for several weeks. Hopefully, this particular storm in a teacup will now blow away.

If anyone in the Blackburn camp is feeling the pressure of the title race, no one is showing it. In fact, it hardly gets a mention. It is one of the unwritten rules of football not to tempt fate by thinking ahead beyond your next game. Our thoughts are focused entirely on the match at Goodison Park and a difficult encounter it promises to be. Since Joe Royle took over they have become a tough outfit to beat on their own patch. But we are eager for action after a lay-off of over a week and we cannot wait to go out and get our campaign underway again.

That hunger immediately surfaces and Chris Sutton scores after just thirteen seconds. It is his first goal since his marriage and some of the lads had begun to suggest he should get a divorce. Within six minutes we are two up as I grab a second goal from a free-kick move which has been worked on at the training ground. Despite our two goal advantage, Everton come storming back at us and Graham Stuart pulls one back with a great chip shot over Tim Flowers' head. A minute later our keeper proves his worth by touching a shot from Stuart Barlow on to the post. We are extremely grateful still to be in front at half-time but there is another ordeal waiting for us in the second half. Everton bombard our goal and we defend with great resilience, much to the annoyance of the Goodison fans who boo us off at the finish. We take that as a compliment rather than a criticism because we have survived a very difficult test of character.

There is one incident in the second half which sums up the attitude in our camp. In a goalmouth scramble there are at least half a dozen Blackburn players ready to throw their bodies in front of the ball to defend the goal. Colin Hendry even attempts to head the ball as it rolls along the ground towards a flying boot. But our attitude at the moment is that we have to be fearless. It is worth getting a bloody nose or a few bumps and bruises when there is a League Championship to be won. We are all prepared to put our necks on the line whenever there are three points at stake. It might not be the most attractive thing to watch but we are at the stage of the season when points are more important than quality performances.

SUNDAY 2ND

I celebrate our six-point lead at the top in style – by creosoting the new fence and enjoying a day in front of the box. There are four live games being screened – Southampton v Tottenham, Napoli v Sampdoria, Liverpool v Bolton and Manchester United v Leeds. But again, I cannot face the agony of watching the United game, so the fence gets an extra coating. Tim Flowers rings me after the final whistle and informs me United have been held to a 0-0 draw. It means we can go eight points clear if we win our game in hand against QPR on Tuesday.

MONDAY 3RD

Alex Ferguson is quoted in the papers as saying the title race is virtually over. No one is fooled by this blatant bit of kidology. We know there is still a long way to go and United will not throw in the towel until it is mathematically impossible for them to catch us. We travel down to London and I decide to help Tony Parkes, Stuart Ripley and the boss, who are racking their brains to solve a crossword puzzle. One clue in particular is troubling them – the name of the saint whose festival day falls on 31st July. Everyone knows I am not exactly a candidate for *Mastermind* and I think they are expecting me to come back with the answer 'Ian St John'. But I have a surprise in store for them. I have noticed that the newspaper carrying the crossword lists a phone number you can call for the correct answers. I nip down to the front of the coach unnoticed and ring on my mobile to get the answer – St Ignatius. When I return and tell them, they are stunned into silence. I leave them shaking their heads in disbelief but let on later where my sudden stroke of genius came from. Their replies are unprintable.

TUESDAY 4TH

There is another tough game in store for us at Loftus Road against a Rangers side who have struck a good spell of form in their bid to banish any thoughts of relegation. It is a fairly dour first half which ends goalless and the home crowd seem as impressed with us as the Everton fans were last Saturday. But we are in a relentless frame of mind again, especially after Chris Sutton gives us a lead early in the second half. He appears to be getting to grips with married life after all. Once we have our noses in front there is no way we are going to relinquish the lead. We have become experts at grinding out results like this and it is a satisfying feeling. We would have settled for four points from these two troublesome away fixtures so a maximum haul leaves us eight points clear of Manchester United. We know we're in the driving seat now but there are still eighteen points to play for and anything can happen.

WEDNESDAY 5TH

Someone forgot to tell the bookies that there is no such thing as a foregone conclusion in football. They have stopped taking bets on us winning the title and, although that is a strong endorsement of our chances, you will not find a single person at Ewood Park agreeing with them.

FRIDAY 7TH

Hardly a week seems to go by without one newspaper or another fixing me up with a transfer to a new club. A report in today's *Daily Express* contains a novel variation on an old theme. It appears that I am bound for Newcastle at the end of the season. Nothing new in that, I agree, but the gist of the story is that an £8.3m bankers draft has already been raised to secure my transfer. It would be fascinating to know where all these stories come from!

I have more urgent matters to deal with after training. My jockey pal Brendan Powell calls me this afternoon to give me some inside information on tomorrow's Grand National. I have a strong fancy for Party Politics but Brendan assures me it has no chance – even less than his own mount Do Be Brief. Dubacilla is the hot tip among the jockeys and I put a few bob each way on it.

My mum and nan are spending the weekend at our house, looking after the kids, because Lainya and I are travelling to London tomorrow for the Professional Footballers' Association awards.

SATURDAY 8TH

I remember to tell Ray Harford during training that I have it on very good authority that his selection for the Grand National, Party Politics, is not worth backing and he thanks me for passing on the advice. After work I meet Lainya at Manchester airport and, during the wait for our flight at Heathrow, we are able to watch the big race on television. So much for Mr Powell's knowledge. Party Politics runs a smashing race and finishes second behind Royal Athelete. I can imagine what Ray will have to say when I meet him at the dinner. I manage to cash in with my each way bet when Dubacilla finishes fourth. The Grand National is a wonderful spectacle but it confirms my opinion that horse-racing is even more precarious than football when it comes to forecasting results.

We check in at the Grosvenor House Hotel and get ready for dinner at Langan's restaurant.

SUNDAY 9TH

The word among the players is that the main PFA award is going to be a close-run thing between myself, Matthew Le Tissier and Jurgen Klinsmann. Just in case I have won, I prepare my acceptance speech and decide to have a bit of fun by quoting from the wise sayings of *Monsieur* Cantona. I intend to say, 'Being a bit of a philosopher myself, I know that the seagulls follow the trawlers because they think sardines are going to be thrown into the sea.' Then I will sit down. I mention this to Kenny Dalglish who is the guest of honour and will be making the main presentation. He thinks it's a great idea – but I have to win it first.

I watch brief snatches of the FA Cup semi-finals on television and am impressed by Everton's emphatic 4-1 win over Tottenham, but Manchester United and Crystal Palace have to replay after a 2-2 draw. Lainya joins a group of other wives for a night on the town while we get down to the serious business of the awards.

Umbro have arranged a table for me, my dad, Lainya's dad, Mike Newell and Jack Hixon and we raise our glasses in celebration when six Blackburn players are named in the Premiership select side – Tim Flowers, Graeme Le Saux, Colin Hendry, Tim Sherwood, Chris Sutton and myself. The young player's prize is presented by Ray Wilkins to Robbie Fowler. I voted for the Liverpool striker myself because I think for him to score goals so consistently at his age and at this level is a wonderful achievement. My vote for the main award was the same as last year. I went for Paul Ince, who has kept the Manchester United team together in what has been a traumatic season for them in many ways. Interestingly, when Eric Cantona's name is read out as one of the nominees there is a brief bout of booing. Obviously he is not top of everyone's popularity poll at the moment.

The gaffer makes his speech and he gets a big laugh from the audience with his reference to seagulls, trawlers and sardines. He reads my name out as the winner and, as I step up to receive the trophy, I whisper to him, 'Thanks for nicking my speech!'

He replies, 'That's quite all right. Now let's hear your effort.' I manage to regather my thoughts as I stand in front of 1,500 people and I receive a round of applause for saying that 'although the image of football has suffered this season, we will succeed in putting the pride back into our game.' I am thrilled to be honoured in this way by my fellow professionals and to see my name among an illustrious list of previous winners. As Kenny Dalglish said in a part of his speech he didn't pinch from me, 'Opponents spend ten months of the year trying to kick you and for them to single you out as the outstanding player in the country is a very special reward.'

I find the awards ceremony a bit nerve-racking but I can now sit back and enjoy myself. Manchester United's late equaliser in the semi-final means we will not now be playing Crystal Palace on Tuesday so I can have an extra glass or two of wine. My dad is a proud man tonight. He even says 'well done' to me. He never usually goes overboard with his praise so I guess this honour means as much to him as it does to me.

Afterwards, Tony gives me a tongue-in-cheek present to mark the occasion – the BBC Basic Italian Language cassette pack!

MONDAY 10TH

It is after three when I finally get to bed, so it is rather a struggle to get up at 6.45 to catch the flight back to Manchester. It's just as well I didn't have too much to drink because there is a 10.30 training session awaiting us. Thankfully it isn't too tough. Ray Harford is a forgiving sort and decides not to take his revenge for my Grand National gaffe.

When I return home there is a message on the answerphone from Jack Walker offering me his congratulations for winning the PFA award. He rings back later in the afternoon and we have a chat. That's just one of the things that makes him such a fine man. He never misses an opportunity to share the joy of your achievements or commiserate over disappointments.

WEDNESDAY 12TH

After training, I spend the rest of the day at the seaside. I travel to Blackpool to record an advert for Sky TV along with Ian Botham, Ian Woosnam and the boxer Prince Naseem Hamed, who turns out to be quite a character. He is only five feet three inches tall and I remark to him that he looks a lot bigger on TV. 'That's because I am usually standing over my opponent with my arms up having knocked him out,' he replies. Confident boy.

In the evening I watch the semi-final replay and there is a shadow hanging over the game because of a fan's death on Sunday. The two managers, Alan Smith and Alex Ferguson, make a special plea for peace to both sets of fans. Unfortunately, it is lost on a few of the players and United's Roy Keane and Palace's Darren Patterson are sent off. Keane can have no arguments with his red card for stamping on Gareth Southgate and Patterson is dismissed for retaliation but I reckon there is an over-the-top response from the media. They want stronger action taken because they claim the two players have scarred a game which had an extra significance. I don't mean to sound in any way disrespectful, especially to the family of the poor man who was killed, but if the sendings-off had occurred in any other game, the players would have served their suspensions and nothing more would have been said. Now they are facing further charges from the Football Association and football has made front page headlines for the wrong reasons yet again.

THURSDAY 13TH

After taking Chloe to nursery, I prepare to do an interview with Gary Lineker for *Football Focus* at our house. He again offers his apologies for his remarks a few weeks age although, as far as I'm concerned, the matter is closed. The BBC crew arrive and the whole interview is only supposed to take an hour or so, but the technicians manage to blow all the electrical fuses and there is a long delay while they fix them. They are unable to get the electronic gate at the end of my drive working, however, and I end up calling in a local electrician who solves the problem in half an hour. I decline to send the bill to the BBC – the TV licence fee is expensive enough without adding to the corporation's costs!

FRIDAY 14TH

An overnight stay in Leeds before tomorrow's match at Elland Road and I get some fearful stick from the other players for yet another interview on Sky. I try to keep quiet about my appearance on *Football Focus* tomorrow but I know I'll be in for some more ribbing. It's true I have been on television a lot recently but that is a reflection of the team's success. There is no jealousy or resentment from my team-mates. They just enjoy taking the mickey. I'm sure they are all aware that I turn down a lot more interview requests than I accept.

SATURDAY 15TH

Our first game in ten days promises to be one of the hardest of the season. It is a fair bet that Manchester United will collect maximum points at Leicester, who are already relegated, so we know we have to pick up at least a point. Before the kick-off the referee Graham Poll congratulates me on winning the PFA award. I thank him and remember that he gave us a penalty in a match against Ipswich earlier this season for a foul on me. 'I wouldn't mind another one of those today,' I remark, only half-joking. He replies, 'I don't think so. Don't forget you were at home that day.' This is rather a strange thing to say but I think no more of it.

Our performance against Leeds is our best for some time – certainly in terms of quality football. We take the lead through a Colin Hendry header and begin passing the ball around accurately and confidently. Unfortunately we don't have any more goals to show for our pressure but, with time running out, we look good for another victory. The 90 minutes are almost up when I cut into the penalty box past David Wetherall, leaving me one-against-one with goalkeeper John Lukic. Suddenly I am upended and it looks like the clearest penalty award you have seen. Mr Poll does not agree and I make my feelings known to both him and his linesman. His pre-match comments flash through my mind. Well, I suppose he stuck to his word, didn't he?

Leeds go straight to the other end, force a corner and Brian Deane equalises with an injury-time header. We feel as flat as pancakes but it is another of those situations where our emotions are mixed. A draw against Leeds away from home is an admirable result but we know it should have been a victory so we feel as if we have been slapped in the face. On the other hand, we have negotiated three successive away games and have collected seven points. United's 4-0 win at Leicester means the gap has been closed to six points and all the talk in the media is that the title race has been opened up again. Funny, I don't remember anyone at Blackburn ever saying it was closed.

SUNDAY 16TH

After a night of tossing and turning and repeating to myself over and over again how many points we would be clear if we had won, I play the whole match again in my head several times. It's like a video machine is running in my head and I cannot switch it off. The penalty incident gets endless action replays and I still can't work out why the referee does not give it. Poor Lainya didn't sleep much either. Such are the perils of being married to a footballer. I know some players take sleeping pills to avoid these sorts of restless nights but I don't want to resort to them. I would hate to become reliant on them.

I cannot wait to ring Tim Flowers and discuss the overall Championship situation. We console each other by agreeing that we are still in pole position and every team in the country would be glad to swap places with us. I know I have to snap out of my despondency because it it Easter Sunday and Lainya's family are spending the weekend with us. I have two young daughters to think about as well and it does not mean a thing to them that Blackburn Rovers have missed the chance to open up their lead at the top of the Premiership. After a good lunch we spend the afternoon in the garden helping Chloe to hunt for the Easter eggs we have hidden. There is a story in the *Sunday Mirror* linking me with a £10m move to AC Milan. I thought my interview with the Italian newspaper would have halted the flow of speculation but it appears not.

MONDAY 17TH

We have a good chance to get Saturday's disappointment out of our system because we are at home against Manchester City tonight and it is the type of game we expect to win. Tim, Mike and I travel into the training ground and I settle for a jacuzzi, a game of pool and a spot of lunch rather than anything too strenuous. We check into the hotel, aware that Manchester United are playing at home against Chelsea and a victory will bring them to within three points of us. Tim comes round to our room and we sit watching the Teletext results. It gets to half-time and the score from Old Trafford is still 0-0. I cannot stand it anymore and at four o'clock I get into the bath. Tim and Mike keep telling me the score and I decide that I will not get out of the bath while the match remains goalless. I have to keep topping it up with hot water and I stay there until 4.45 p.m. when the final result comes through. United have been held and our spirits are soaring again. Now we can take full advantage by beating City and I doubt whether there will be a cleaner footballer on the pitch after my marathon session in the tub.

When we arrive at Ewood Park there is an incredible feeling around the place. I do not think I have seen our supporters in such a celebratory mood all season. When we run out for our warm-up before the kick-off there is a carnival atmosphere waiting for us. You would think we had already won the Championship. There are two ways this can affect a team. It can either fill you with so much confidence you feel it is impossible to lose, or it can generate so much confidence that you become complacent. I think the latter reason is the case today, even though I give us an early lead by cashing in on a poor clearance from the City goalkeeper Tony Coton.

But our opponents need points as well to climb away from the relegation zone and they begin playing out of their skins. They force their way back into the game by equalising with a Keith Curle penalty which is awarded when Ian Pearce is ruled to have pulled back Niall Quinn. Colin Hendry puts us ahead again just before half-time but we are still not performing as well as we can. City draw level again through Uwe Rosler and Paul Walsh scores a third to put them ahead. That leaves us with what we deserve – absolutely nothing – but let us not take anything away from our opponents. They played at a sustained high level which must have surprised even their own supporters. For this game we wear black armbands and hold a minute's silence to mark the death of Mick Heaton, who was a very popular coach at Blackburn when Howard Kendall was manager.

At the final whistle you would have thought the armbands were to commemorate the passing of our Championship hopes. There is an eerie silence in the dressing-room which is a complete contrast to the buzz and banter which was flying around before the game started. No one says anything but we know there is only one solution. We have all got to roll up our sleeves and work even harder, starting with Thursday's game against Crystal Palace.

On the way home Tim, Mike and I try to look on the bright side by reminding ourselves that this was only our fifth defeat of the season and, with only four games remaining, we are still five points clear. But are we clutching at straws?

TUESDAY 18TH

Another sleepless night leaves me feeling drained as well as dejected. I know I will feel much better physically after ten hours sleep but will my mind ever get right? Yet when we get into the training ground for a jacuzzi and a massage, the mood among the players is surprisingly buoyant with plenty of laughing and joking. It says a lot for the team's spirit that we can survive such a result with our heads up. You never know, the defeat might just have given us the jolt we need for the final push.

In the afternoon I take the dog for a long walk, and start thinking again of what might have been if we had won last night. My head is full of ifs, buts and maybes. I seem to get into this frame of mind when I am on my own. I promised Lainya we would take her family out for dinner tonight if we had beaten Manchester City but she persuades me to go anyway and it does me good to think about something other than football.

WEDNESDAY 19TH

Colin Hendry and Tim Sherwood will miss tomorrow's game through suspensions and it becomes clear today that David Batty and Kevin Gallacher will play their first full senior games of the season. David has been out for a year and Kevin for fifteen months and they are both bursting to play a part in this memorable season. Their enthusiasm is bound to rub off on the rest of us. Lainya's mum and dad and brother Gareth travel home to Southampton today. I bet they're glad to see the back of me after the way I've been moping around the house for the last few days.

THURSDAY 20TH

A bath and a game of pool followed by an afternoon nap satisfy my requirements before the Palace game. The mood at Ewood is understandably a lot more subdued than on Monday. I think our fans are as nervous as the players about this game. The absence of Tim and Colin means we are without our skipper and his deputy, so Kenny Dalglish asks me just before the kick-off how I feel about captaining the side. I say I would love to and he gives me the armband. When the other lads see me putting it on, they think there is another minute's silence planned before the match. I regard it as a real honour. I was captain of Southampton for a spell when I was twenty and I thrived on the extra responsibility. I hope it will have the same effect on me tonight.

We start off as though we cannot wait to get our last two results out of our system. David Batty performs as though he has never been out of the team and reminds us what a good player he is. He adds an extra dimension to our game because he is always available to receive the ball. While we have been hitting it forward to the strikers quite quickly for most of the season, David gives us a bit more variety. He can pick it up from the back four and can pass five, ten or fifteen yards to build our attacks more precisely. Jeff Kenna, who has moved to right back from midfield to cover Henning Berg's switch to the centre of the defence, puts us ahead with his first goal for the club. I do not remember much about the move but I do know Jeff puts it away like a good 'un. The relief is such that he is submerged under a mass of bodies as we celebrate the goal. Kevin Gallacher looks lively out on the left and it is a reward for his determination and patience in overcoming his injury when he adds a second goal. Then tragedy strikes Kevin again. He is brought down by a bad tackle from John Humphrey and is carried off with another suspected leg fracture. Humphrey is lucky to escape with a yellow rather than a red card and is substituted soon afterwards.

Poor Kevin heads for hospital for X-rays with his season over almost before it has begun. Palace pull a goal back through Ray Houghton with a quarter of an hour left and our nerve ends are exposed again. We should be well in front by now but face an anxious finale and Tim Flowers saves the three points for us by pushing a shot from our former Southampton team-mate Iain Dowie on to the post. We have learned our lesson from the Leeds game, however, and manage to keep possession of the ball through the closing few minutes to deny Palace any further chances.

I enjoy a drink or two in the players' lounge with Iain Dowie and, before heading for home, Mike Newell and I treat ourselves to a McChicken sandwich and chips as a reward for our win.

FRIDAY 21ST

Still no sleep last night but at least my mind is full of happier thoughts. The morning newspapers confirm that we now need five more points from our three remaining matches to be sure of the title. It might be less if United drop any points from their remaining four games but we must assume they will win the lot to guard against further complacency.

Lainya, myself and the kids join the Flowers family for lunch. Needless to say I pay again!

SATURDAY 22ND

I wake up with a sore head. It was Mike Newell's brother Steve's stag do last night and Mike, Tim Flowers and I joined him and his mates for a knees-up. After a meal and a few pubs we ended up in a nightclub where we enjoyed a few more drinks. As per usual, Tim left early on his own without even saying goodbye. We all went home at around 1.30 a.m. slightly the worse for wear but not totally incapable. I think it did me good because it took my mind off football and the chase for the Championship.

We are all entitled to a bit of a fling occasionally, especially as we are not playing this weekend. There are no Premiership fixtures because of the international programme next week, though England have been unable to arrange a friendly. Terry Venables has called together a group of players for a training session but no one from teams involved in the Championship or relegation matches takes part. This allows him the chance to have a closer look at some of the fringe candidates like Stan Collymore, Steve Stone and Mark Draper. It has left the rest of us at a loose end, however, and I am sure I speak for the majority of players when I say we would rather be in action.

The whole fixture list is topsy-turvy at the moment. After playing three games in six days we have a wait of ten days before we face West Ham tomorrow week. Such a big gap between matches gives a team no chance to build up any momentum. We were glad of the opportunity to play Crystal Palace so soon after the Manchester City defeat because it gave us an immediate chance to get a bad performance out of our systems. We could have done with a game this week while we are back on song. The rest is nice but we are itching to get going again. There is only one way for me to spend this Saturday off – flat on my back on the settee, nursing my headache and watching the horse-racing on television. To make amends for our night out with the boys, Tim, Mike and I have agreed to take our wives out for an Italian meal tonight and it is a much more civilised occasion than 24 hours ago.

SUNDAY 23RD

Chloe and Hollie get their turn for a treat today and after a morning at the swimming baths, we visit McDonalds. In the afternoon I look forward to seeing Paul Gascoigne in action in the big derby game between Lazio and Roma on Channel Four but he is only named as one of the substitutes. I get fed up waiting for him to be sent on and take the dog for a walk before the match ends.

Gazza has always fascinated me as a player and a person. I was just about to join Southampton as an apprentice when he broke into the Newcastle first team and it was clear from the outset that he was a frightening football talent. I have got to know him as part of the England set-up and can vouch for the fact that he is crazy. He will do anything for a laugh and a joke, though many of his pranks are unprintable. He has suffered cruel luck with injuries, having broken his leg soon after getting over his serious knee ligament problem. You always sense Gazza is an accident waiting to happen. He is so pumped up before games that he goes steaming into challenges and is often too brave for his own good. I just hope he will enjoy an injury-free spell now and show the world the remarkable ability he still has at his command.

MONDAY 24TH

We are back in training today but our next game seems a long way off. This feels odd because it is the time of the season when you expect the matches to come thick and fast. I think quite a few of us are already feeling restless. As hard as I try it is not easy to rid my mind of what could yet happen in the Championship race. The newspapers are full of it and so are the television stations. I just wish the talking would stop and we could get on with the real business of winning points again.

TUESDAY 25TH

I spend the afternoon in Huddersfield helping to promote their friendly against Blackburn at the start of next season. I also do an interview with a journalist for the new Football Association magazine which is being launched this summer. When I get home I hear some unbelievably bad news. Paul Warhurst has broken his leg in training and this is a tragic blow for our Mr Versatile. He has had bad luck of Gazza-style proportions since joining us from Sheffield Wednesday. He broke his leg last season, fought his way back and has now suffered a similar injury in the other leg. It is also confirmed that Kevin Gallacher has a hairline fracture and will be out until the start of pre-season training.

WEDNESDAY 26TH

After training today, I go to Ewood Park to sort out some post and sign some autograph requests, when I discover the club have a surprise in store for me. They present me with a framed photograph of me scoring my 100th goal which I am delighted with. I have another interview for the *News of the World* scheduled for this weekend and I meet up with their reporter during the afternoon. They want me to reveal the nicknames of my colleagues in a light-hearted look at the characters within the Blackburn dressing-room but I do not think it is very appropriate at this tense stage of the season. In the end I agree to talk about Jack Walker and how down-to-earth and friendly he is to every single person at Blackburn Rovers from the players to the tea lady.

THURSDAY 27TH

I spend the first couple of hours of another day off taking the dog for a walk. It is a superb day – perfect weather for Steve Newell's wedding. Mike is his best man and I can't wait to hear his speech. I am ready to give him loads of stick because he is always going on about me being on TV all the time and boring everyone with my interviews. But, to be honest, I cannot fault his performance today. I can tell he is nervous but he gets through without any serious mishaps.

FRIDAY 28TH

Eric Cantona has announced that he is staying at Manchester United and that is a real shot in the arm for them because the speculation over recent weeks has been that he was going to join Inter Milan. He could probably have earned himself a lot more money by moving to Italy but he has shown his loyalty to United. We will have to wait until next season to see what effect the whole affair will have on his relationship with the English football public. I have noticed in one or two games recently that there has been an outbreak of booing from opposition supporters when United fans have chanted his name. I can see he will face a hostile reaction when he starts playing again – not only from the terraces but out on the pitch. Certain players are bound to try to wind him up and he will have to show a lot of restraint and self-control. Having said that, he is a tremendous player and would have been a big loss to Manchester United and the Premiership as a whole.

I find United captain Steve Bruce's interview on Sky Television tonight rather fascinating. He goes on and on about the long injury list which they have had to contend with this season and some United fans also refer to the suspension of Cantona as a turning point in the Championship race. I don't know whether this is an attempt to lull us into complacency or is aimed at putting pressure on us. I feel sure we would be doing the same if the roles were reversed. However, when it comes to injuries I would just like to point out that we have been without David Batty and Kevin Gallacher for most of the season and Paul Warhurst, Jason Wilcox and Mike Newell for a sizeable part of the campaign. That adds up to about £12m worth of talent sidelined at various stages – it seems that both United and ourselves have been dealt bad hands in the casualty stakes. Injuries are part and parcel of the game, and so it is no good complaining about them.

SATURDAY 29TH

Before travelling to London for tomorrow's game against West Ham, Rovers chairman, Robert Coar, pulls me to one side and tells me that Jurgen Klinsmann has been voted the Football Writers' Association's Player of the Year with me in second place and Colin Hendry in third. I always suspected the top spot would be a close-run thing between the three of us and I take my hat off to the German international. He has performed magnificently for Spurs and has done himself proud despite all the odds being stacked against him at first. When he arrived there the mere mention of his name used to provoke cries of 'cheat' and 'diver' but he has won over the supporters of many clubs with his ability and attitude. He has been good for the game off the field as well with his handling of the public and the Press. I am not disappointed at failing to retain the award which I won last year. I have the PFA award for my collection and if I can get my hands on the biggest honour of all – the Premiership trophy – I will be more than satisfied. The title race is still nagging away at my thoughts. D Day is fast approaching and some people are claiming that a victory over the Hammers will put us beyond United's reach. We will only believe that when they do not have enough games to overhaul our points total.

SUNDAY 30TH

A headline in the *News of the World* this morning tells readers that Alan Shearer is staying at Blackburn. Strange, I do not remember ever saying I was going anywhere. The background to the story reveals how sometimes facts can become distorted. It began when the local paper in Blackburn, the *Lancashire Evening Telegraph*, carried an interview with Jack Walker in which he said he would love me to sign a new contract taking me beyond the one which expires at the end of next season. The *News of the World* reporter, Paul Hetherington, rang me to ask for my reaction to this and I said I would have to discuss it with the Rovers chairman first because I did not want to conduct any negotiations through the Press. Mr Coar was happy for me to go ahead and talk about Mr Walker's remarks and my response to the *News of the World* was, 'If Blackburn want to discuss a new deal with me, I will be more than happy to sit down and have talks with them.' That is somewhat different from saying, 'I am staying with Rovers.' It just goes to show that a wrong headline and false emphasis can be very misleading.

The truth is that I will gladly listen to what the club have to say and talks will probably take place during the summer. If there is an offer on the table I will take my time and consider it carefully, but all this can wait. There is the simple matter of a Championship to be won and all my attention is being taken up by that at present.

We are bright and lively from the kick-off without ever threatening to open up the West Ham defence. As the match unfolds it begins to remind me of the two legs of our UEFA Cup clash against Trelleborg. They get plenty of men behind the ball, make it difficult for us to break them down and then hit us powerfully and effectively on the counter-attack. The atmosphere at Upton Park is very intimidating with the crowd very close to the action, and the temperature starts to rise as tackles go flying in from both sides. That is only to be expected with us chasing Championship points and West Ham scrapping for their Premiership future.

We suffer a setback early in the second half when Marc Rieper heads West Ham in front but I force the ball in after an aerial collison between Chris Sutton and Ludek Miklosko only for it to be disallowed for a foul on the West Ham goalkeeper. It is another decision which I find baffling. When a keeper tries to reach the ball over the head of an attacker and the opponent just stands his ground I cannot see how there can be an infringement, but I suppose we live in an age where goalies are a protected species. I discuss it with some West Ham people afterwards and, after seeing it on TV, it is widely agreed that the 'goal' should have counted.

The Hammers deal us another blow late in the game when Don Hutchison adds a second goal but, by that time, we have fully committed ourselves to chasing an equaliser with four men in attack and our defence exposed to the breakaway. There is no way back for us now and it is a very disconsolate group of players who leave the pitch to reflect on the fact that we have now taken just four points from our last four games. That is not Championship form and we know it but let us not forget that we built ourselves some insurance against this happening with our tremendous form at the start of the run-in. The gaffer puts it all into perspective when he tell us, 'It is still in our hands and if we want it badly enough no one will stop us. We have two games left against Newcastle and Liverpool and we can win them both. We have come this far, so why throw it away now?' He also reminds us that the League table shows that we are still eight points clear of United, who have two games in hand, and we are not there by any fluke. We are in that position because, over the duration of the season, we have been the best team in the country and now we have two matches left to confirm it.

The boss tells us he does not want to see us in for training until Thursday and advises us not to get involved with any Press articles which try to suggest the team is cracking up or that we have bottled it. We are heartened by his words but it is still a fairly quiet journey home. Somewhere along the M6 our progress is delayed by a road accident and we see a woman lying by the side of the road. She is clearly in a serious condition and it is a sobering sight. Why should we be feeling sorry for ourselves when there are people suffering from far more critical problems than we are?

MAY 1995

MONDAY 1ST

I am up at 7.30 a.m. and take Chloe out for the morning to feed the ducks and swans before joining Mike Newell on the golf course. I beat him on the final hole which means he has to dip into his pocket and pay for the round. It is a good time to be playing him, though, because he has just taken delivery of his new BMW car and seems to be in a hurry to get home for a drive in it.

I notice on Teletext later that David Batty and Tim Sherwood could be charged by the Football Association for challenges they made during the West Ham game. As far as David's tackle was concerned, it was late and he probably deserved to get booked but it was no worse than the one on Chris Sutton which earned Julian Dicks a caution. Tim caught Don Hutchison with a flying elbow but, again, I do not believe there was anything malicious involved. It was a game with so much at stake that you were bound to get total commitment and a few bumps and bruises. West Ham's Hutchison and Jeroen Boere finished up with broken noses, Colin Hendry with a gashed eye and me with a swollen mouth but no one from either side complained. That's the way it should be and I am surprised that the FA has got involved.

Manchester United's game at Coventry is live on Sky and I have to admit I am not brave enough to watch it all. I keep flicking over to the other channels whenever United are on the attack but manage to catch the goals in the highlights later which show a 3-2 victory for the men from Old Trafford. To be honest we expected them to go there and win. They got a bit of help from two defensive mistakes but Andy Cole took his two goals well and they deserved their victory.

The pressure is really on us now. Five points separate us and they still have an extra game to play. It wouldn't surprise me if it goes to the final day of the season when we visit Liverpool and United are at West Ham. We hope to have wrapped it up before them, but if it does go to the wire I am sure the Hammers will be just as committed against them as they were against us.

TUESDAY 2ND

It is a glorious summer day and I am determined not to spoil it by dwelling too much on what might still happen in our remaining games. After a morning shopping for clothes with Lainya in Liverpool, I spend the afternoon in the garden with my family and the world of football seems a million miles away.

WEDNESDAY 3RD

I have planned a round of golf with Neil Ruddock today but, to my dismay, I saw on Teletext last night that he had to go off with a hamstring injury during Liverpool's goalless draw at Wimbledon. However, he rings me up quite early to tell me that it does not feel too bad and he might still be able to join me after he has been in for treatment. Then he calls again later to say that the club has insisted he goes to see a specialist about the groin injury which has been troubling him, and our game is off again. Neil learns later that he has to have a hernia operation so his season has come to an abrupt end. This is a pity because we had worked out a suitable climax to the campaign. If we still needed a win in our final match on Sunday week against Liverpool and the scores were level, he was going to trip me up in the penalty area in the final few minutes. Only joking! I can assure you that we would never pull a trick like that. Neil is a tough competitor who hates losing so much that he would have done everything in his power to stop us from winning the title.

I still owe him one for the way he trampled all over me at Ewood Park so I suppose I will have to wait until next season to pay him back.

Now that my golf day has been ruined I take the dog for a walk. The good weather has brought the day-trippers out in force and, for the first time this year, the beach is packed with people. I know a few remote spots off the beaten track so Candy and I still manage to enjoy some peace and quiet away from the crowds.

Tim Flowers joins me at the Blackburn Disabled Supporters' Player of the Year presentation tonight and I am delighted to have topped their poll.

THURSDAY 4TH

We are back in training after our prolonged break and the rest has cured the hangover we were suffering immediately after the West Ham defeat. We all realise we were rubbish that day and the performance and result are best forgotten. After training I attend a photo shoot to illustrate the interview I have already done for the Football Association's new magazine and, on my way home, Mike Newell rings me on the car phone to invite the family round to his house for the first barbecue of the summer.

FRIDAY 5TH

Tony Stephens calls and tells me that a company is compiling an unauthorised video about me. Apparently they are doing an official one on Matthew Le Tissier and among the footage they have obtained is some action of me scoring goals for Southampton. It transpires they are also trying to acquire some film of me playing for England as part of the package which will be entitled 'A Tribute to Alan Shearer'. It seems that the cover will state that it is unauthorised and apparently, there is very little we can do to stop it coming out which I find extremely annoying. If kids are being offered material with my name attached to it, I want it to be high quality and not hastily cobbled together. It is wrong that young fans should be exploited by a company who have not received my permission or co-operation in the production of their video, which will not feature any of my home goals for Blackburn. We have contacted the FA about the situation so that they will hopefully try and close this loophole in the future.

I receive more disturbing information about a supposed interview with me in a magazine called *Premier Megastars*. Most of it is made up of quotations and remarks I have made in other articles. They have been collected and presented in a way which suggests I have actually spoken to someone from the magazine. I have not. This is bad enough but they have taken an even bigger liberty. I am supposed to have been asked what it was like to have won the title and am reported as saying, 'It feels great and Manchester United have pushed us all the way.' Clearly the publishers have printed the May edition of the magazine early and have gambled on us clinching the Championship before it hits the streets. Now that is way out of order. Even if they had asked for a quote in advance and told me they would only use it when the title was won I would not have given them one. I do not like taking anything for granted. The fact that they have quoted me without even having the courtesy to speak to me only makes matters worse. I complain to them and receive an apology but am still not satisfied and have now lodged a formal protest with the Press Complaints Commission. I am angry about it because it not only makes me look foolish by putting words which I have not said into my mouth, but it is another example of kids being ripped off. They will buy the magazine in good faith, expecting it to contain original information when it is in fact second-hand and inaccurate.

Just to improve my mood I pick up an injury in training. I go up for a header with Colin Hendry, land on his leg and turn my left ankle over. I have to make a speedy exit to the medical room for ice-pack treatment. But I am fit enough later to take Chloe to Children's World to buy her a trampoline. My mum and dad are spending the weekend with us and staying for Monday's game against Newcastle. Dad agrees to help me put the trampoline together – a job which, according to the instructions, should take no more than 45 minutes. After two hours we are still outside in the dark, wrestling with the various parts. The thing about my dad is that he will not listen to those who know best. I wonder why he says exactly the same about me.

SATURDAY 6TH

The boss asks us whether we want to train tomorrow morning or in the afternoon. If we leave it until after lunch we can avoid having to sit through Manchester United's television game against Sheffield Wednesday. The majority view is that we have no need to change our routine and several of the lads want to watch the match anyway. I am afraid I will not be one of them. I have more treatment on my ankle but it feels a lot better and there is no way I intend missing the Newcastle match.

SUNDAY 7TH

I manage to complete a full training session with the ankle strapped up and after lunch I settle down to watch the football on the TV. No, not the United-Wednesday match but the First Divison clash between Tranmere and Middlesbrough and the Juventus-Lazio game from Italy. Dad watches United in action in another room but is under strict instructions not to tell me the result until it finishes. He breaks the news after 90 minutes that they have won 1-0 with a goal from our former defender David May. Anything other than a United win would have been a major upset and, apparently, Wednesday only launched one serious attack on their goal. It brings United to within two points of us and we have both played 40 matches. Now that is what you call pressure. We know we are capable of beating Newcastle but it is going to be a real test of our character tomorrow night.

MONDAY 8TH

Alex Ferguson tries to turn the screw on our nerve ends with his comments in the morning newspapers: 'Once your form goes you seem to become helpless. In that position you cannot do anything about it.' He is an experienced campaigner and has been playing these mind games with us for a few weeks but no one is paying much attention. We are too busy concentrating on the task facing us and we have a clear vision of what we must achieve tonight. If we do not beat Kevin Keegan's team then the Championship might well slip through our fingers. Even a draw could mean the end of the road for us because that would leave United three points behind with a game in hand and a superior goal difference. It is the 50th anniversary of Victory in Europe today but we have our own VE mission to accomplish – Victory at Ewood. Nothing else will do.

On the way into the ground I notice a banner in Rovers' colours draped over a bridge. It reads 'No Surrender' – a very appropriate slogan for the battle ahead of us. The *Lancashire Evening Telegraph* has put out a message to fans to support the team tonight like they have never done before. The rallying call does not go unanswered. There are over 30,000 fans in the stadium and they create a fantastic atmosphere.

Before the match starts I have a couple of presentations to attend. The first is to receive the Golden Boot award which goes to the Premiership's highest scorer. I feel a little bit uneasy because, as I have said before, I do not like jumping the gun and taking anything for granted. There are still two games left and Liverpool's Robbie Fower is seven goals behind me. While it is unlikely he will overhaul my total, I do not like the idea of receiving the prize before the season ends. But I cannot attend the formal presentation on Sunday night, so I have agreed to help out by taking part in an unofficial ceremony.

I do not mind for one minute receiving my second award of the evening. I have been voted Player of the Year by the Blackburn Rovers supporters and I have to go out on to the pitch to receive my award from Jack Walker. To a deafening roar he says that I have been 'the making of the new Blackburn Rovers' and insists he wants to keep me. That is very flattering and Mr Walker knows I have never said I want to leave the club. He is also aware that I will be pleased to talk to him about the future.

The prospect of being involved in a night like this is the main reason why I joined Rovers in the first place. The atmosphere is quite the best I have known since I joined. The noise from our fans is overpowering but they have the opportunity to show they are fair-minded, caring people as well. There is a minute's silence to mark the death of former Blackburn star Noel Brotherston before we kick off and a two-minute tribute as part of the VE celebrations at half-time. On both occasions you can hear a pin drop. But once the action starts, the volume is pumped up to full blast as we give Newcastle a roasting in the early stages. We need a goal to confirm our supremacy and it comes when Graeme Le Saux delivers a gem of a cross for me to head into the net. My momentum carries me into Newcastle full back John Beresford but referee Phil Don dismisses any thoughts of a foul. We are well in command but Tim Flowers still has to pull off an astonishing save to keep out a blistering shot from Peter Beardsley. If that's a top drawer save there is more to follow. Tim produces three more world class stops to keep us ahead including a miraculous one to deny Beresford. This is England's number one keeper in action and, if anyone doubts the wisdom of paying £2m for a goalkeeper, then they should watch Tim in this form.

While Newcastle dominate the second half, we still have enough chances to build on our head. Three of them fall to me but I miss the target with one and Pavel Srnicek saves the other two. I expected to put at least a couple of them away. Maybe the tension has got to me – I know I should have sewn the game up. If we don't win, I'll blame myself, but there is no time to feel any guilt now. When anxiety creeps in, it has a draining effect on a player, both physically and mentally, and stupid mistakes start to occur. We are fortunate to cling on to our lead and the Rovers fans know it. There is a period of about ten or fifteen minutes towards the end when Newcastle seem to be on the attack constantly. Our supporters are stunned into silence, unable to utter a single sound. There is a heart-stopping moment when Colin Hendry tackles Keith Gillespie and the Newcastle winger goes down in a heap in the area but Mr Don, quite rightly, refuses a penalty. Soon afterwards the ball goes out of play behind Tim's goal. For a moment the relentless pressure on our goal is over and the eruption of sound is ear-shattering. The fans know we have weathered the storm.

At the final whistle the relief is incredible. What do we do now? We have picked up three points from our final game of the season at Ewood Park but dare not show too much exuberance in case we are accused of prematurely celebrating the title. We talk about it in the dressing-room afterwards and agree that we have to go out and show our appreciation to the fans but must tone down our reaction. Normally we would do a lap of honour in our last home game but we settle for a wave from the centre circle. It is a pity we cannot be too demonstrative because our fans have shown tonight they are capable of a passion and level of support we did not think possible. Let us see them sustain it from now on. Lainya, Mum and Dad and Jack Hixon are watching the match and that makes it even more special. Also David Platt and Sampdoria captain Roberto Mancini have flown over in a private jet to see the game prior to watching David's new horse, Il Doria, run for the first time at Chester tomorrow. Eventually I make my way home, emotionally drained but knowing full well I will not sleep tonight.

TUESDAY 9TH

I stay up until 2.30 a.m. to watch the second showing of the match on Sky and then relive the highlights hundreds of times as I lie awake in bed. I think I slip off to sleep some time after four o'clock but rise at 7.30 ready for a game of golf with Mike Newell. He has joined a new golf and country club called Portal in Cheshire and it is very impressive, with two courses amid very luxurious surroundings. The chairman, Mr Taylor, recognises me before we go out and says he would like a chat when we have completed our round. Mike beats me on the last hole after which Mr Taylor is kind enough to offer me a celebrity membership. The list already includes Kenny Dalglish, Alan Hansen, Mike

Newell, Dean Saunders, Ian Rush, snooker player John Parrott and comic Stan Boardman – so it is a compliment to be included in such company and I am delighted to accept.

I briefly watch the racing on television in the afternoon and David's horse comes in second at 4/1. He is interviewed before the race and sounds more knowledgeable about horses than his trainer, Jack Berry.

Lainya and I go out for a meal with Neil and Sarah Ruddock tonight and, unfortunately, I am unable to unearth any secrets about how we can topple Liverpool on Sunday. They have received a pasting in the Press from their manager, Roy Evans, after a lacklustre display against Aston Villa last Saturday so I think we can expect the backlash at Anfield.

WEDNESDAY 10TH

There is a choice for us at training. We can either take part in a full session or settle for a gentle jog and a soak in the bath. I choose the easier option because I am not feeling too well. I have a sore throat and feel a little feverish so I dash home and go straight to bed. I get up for something to eat in the early evening and settle down to watch Arsenal play Real Zaragoza in the European Cup-Winners' Cup final. The Manchester United-Southampton match is completely off-limits as far as I'm concerned. I do not have to bother ringing up any of my old mates from The Dell to recruit their help because I know they will do everything within their power to deny United victory and give us the Championship. It will be quite something if Neil Maddison, Tommy Widdrington and Matthew Le Tissier can play a part because we shared so many good times when we were growing up together as young Saints.

I take all my phones off the hook in case anyone attempts to ring me with a progress report from Old Trafford. I do not want to know anything about the game until it's over. Lainya decides to watch the match on a TV upstairs, but I insist she takes a vow of silence until the final whistle. I watch the Arsenal game but, to be honest, I am not really taking too much of it in because my mind keeps wandering to what might be happening to United.

Lainya comes down at half-time and I can see there is a slight grin on her face. 'Come on then, you'd better tell me what's happening,' I say to her. She informs me that Southampton have taken the lead after five minutes through Simon Charlton and are playing really well but Andy Cole has equalised. So far so good, though I still cannot bear to watch the second half. I can't concentrate on the Arsenal match either and I receive a jolt when the score from Old Trafford flashes on to the screen – Manchester United 2, Southampton 1. I look at my watch and see there are less than ten minutes remaining and suspect there is no way back for the Saints now. Lainya comes downstairs and, again, I can tell by the look on her face what the final result is. I discover later that Denis Irwin scored from the penalty spot after Ken Monkou was penalised for fouling Andy Cole. When I watch the replay I am convinced it is a harsh decision. It is the sort of incident that occurs in every single game but the referee Paul Danson awards the spot-kick and our agony goes on. Eight minutes from the title. That is how close we have come to clinching it tonight and it is becoming a slow torture. But we know now that we cannot rely on anyone else to do the job for us. And why should we? The destiny of the Championship is still in our own hands. All we have to do is beat Liverpool at Anfield on Sunday and it does not matter how United get on at West Ham.

THURSDAY 11TH

We have been given a day off today but I would not have been able to train anyway. I still feel under the weather and decide to visit the doctor who gives me some penicillin and tells me not to drink alcohol under any circumstances. I have no intention of touching a drop before Sunday – but I might just make up for it after that . . . It crosses my mind that this virus might keep me out of Sunday's game but it is only a fleeting thought. Even if I have a broken leg they will have to tie me down to stop me playing.

FRIDAY 12TH

I miss training again but feel a bit better. My main concern is that I have promised to be at a ceremony in Blackburn where a set of gates is being commemorated in memory of a Rovers' fan who has recently passed away. The organisers are more than satisfied when Tim Flowers and Mike Newell agree to stand in for me. I spend most of the day in bed but the newspapers, radio and TV are full of the Championship race so I can't take my mind off it.

Tim Flowers rings me later with some worrying news. He, Tim Sherwood and the gaffer have received some letters, posted in Scandinavia, threatening they will be killed if Rovers win the title. We agree the best thing to do is to ignore them but it naturally concerns us and the police have been informed. I do not know if I have been sent one because I have not been able to collect my mail from Ewood Park. I would rather not find out for the time being.

SATURDAY 13TH

I am fully recovered and join in a full training session. My seven-a-side team end the season with a rare defeat but we have already won more than enough games to claim the unofficial Blackburn mini-title. That's one in the bag. Now for the big one. We are staying in a hotel overnight but have switched from the one we used recently for the Everton game because the night before that fixture there was a disco going on well into the night which disturbed our sleep. The decision to change was not a good one because this hotel in Warrington is even worse. It feels as if we are sleeping in a nightclub, the noise is so loud. I ring down to reception and discover that there is a stag night in progress. I reckon they must all be Manchester United fans and Alex Ferguson has paid for their entertainment. I am still bopping in my bed at midnight but manage to fall asleep soon afterwards after a silent prayer for a little bit of luck tomorrow.

We certainly do not expect any favours from the opposition. There have been rumours going around that Liverpool will not be going flat out against us because they hate the thought of their old enemies from Old Trafford winning a third successive title. No one in our camp is taking any notice of that. It is a slur against Liverpool to suggest that they will deliberately not try. As one of the biggest clubs in the world, they have a reputation to uphold and their supporters would not stand for anything less than 100 per cent commitment. Nor should it be any other way.

SUNDAY 14TH

I wake at 9.30 a.m. and have it fixed in my mind that my preparations should remain as normal as possible. After a bowl of cornflakes and a cup of tea, I make my normal calls to Lainya, my mum and dad and Jack Hixon and receive their good luck messages down the telephone line. Jack does not have a Sky dish so will not be able to watch the match on TV. He's not a great radio listener so he will watch the results as they come up on Teletext.

I cannot think of a more agonising way of spending an afternoon. After our pre-match meal, the gaffer calls us together for our final team talk of the season. It is a routine outline of what to expect from the opposition with a particular warning to be on our guard against Steven McManaman who tends to roam anywhere along the front line and needs to be picked up by the nearest defender. The boss's final few words are carefully chosen and reinforce everything we need to know. 'We are where we are today on merit,' he declares. 'For 41 games this season we have been the best team in the country. Now let's make it 42. You have done yourselves proud. With one last team effort it can be a day to remember.'

As we travel to the game it becomes obvious that Liverpool fans, for once, have divided loyalties. They do not want United to win the title and I gather there has been a massive sale of Blackburn shirts to fans on Merseyside. One banner catches my eye as we approach the ground. It reads: 'A life-long Liverpool fan but for one day – a Rover.' When we run out for our warm-up, we receive a great ovation from the fans of both teams which is slightly unreal. The injured Neil Ruddock pops into the dressing-room beforehand to pick up a couple of tickets I have promised him. In return he promises us three points but there is no way he can deliver that. He also insists that the champagne will be waiting for us at the final whistle.

The events at Upton Park will be just as crucial to us as those at Anfield but there are no special plans to relay news of the United score. I would rather not know. It is important to remember that we are in the driving seat and if we concentrate on our own task then the prize cannot be taken from us. For the first twenty minutes of the game, we cannot get the ball off Liverpool which immediately destroys the myth that they are going to let us walk all over them. Nigel Clough has an effort cleared off the line by Tim Sherwood and we realise we are right up against it. However, I manage to ease the tension by converting a cross from Stuart Ripley and some ten minutes later there is another huge roar from the crowd from which we assume West Ham have scored. Another cheer from the terraces later suggests the Hammers have scored another but we discover at half-time they are only one goal ahead. If only someone could wind the clocks on 45 minutes and put us out of our misery. But there is still a lot of football to be played. Liverpool take control again in the second half and John Barnes equalises. Unknown to us, United have equalised as well and the Championship could not be more dramatically poised. Chris Sutton misses a good chance and I put a shot over the bar when I should have scored. How costly will this be? What is happening at Upton Park? The questions remain unanswered. When our physiotherapist Steve Foster comes on to the pitch to treat Chris Sutton, we ask him the United score, but he refuses to tell us. From his response, I assume that they are winning but as he is about to run off he informs us it is still 1-1 with eight minutes left. We know that a draw or a defeat for us will make no difference to the outcome. It all hinges on United's result.

Deep in injury time, Jamie Redknapp scores with a free kick from 25 yards to give Liverpool victory. Everything suddenly goes into slow motion. It must only be a matter of seconds but it seems like a couple of hours as we put the ball on the centre spot ready to restart the game. I turn round to knock it back to Tim Sherwood and see that he is jumping up in the air. What is going on? Our match is still in progress but no one seems interested. I look over towards our bench and the gaffer and Ray Harford have their arms around each other. Is it true? Have we really done it? Are we the new Champions? Yes! Sky have two TV sets in the tunnel area and have passed on the news that United's game has finished at 1-1, just a few seconds after Redknapp's goal. Referee David Elleray blows his whistle for the end of our game and we get final confirmation of the United result. The title is ours by a single, solitary, precious point. Anfield erupts in an explosion of blue and red. The celebrations begin and we dance, sing, embrace and do all the delirious things which make grown men look so foolish.

We return briefly to the dressing-room where Ruddock has kept his promise. He is waiting with champagne and beer. I grab a bottle of bubbly and am about to spray it over everyone when, in full view of the TV cameras, Neil trips me up – not for the first time this season. I don't spill a drop. I am shoved before the cameras for an interview but am too overwhelmed to make any sense. The other lads pelt me with beer, champagne, shorts, socks, jockstraps and anything else they can lay their hands on. Tim Flowers tells me later it is one of the less boring interviews I have given.

Back on the pitch, the official presentation takes place and we all raise the trophy in turn before we pose for group photographs. I take a long look at my medal. I have yearned for this moment – not just for the last nine months – for all of my career. Jack Walkers appears on the pitch, having had trouble initially finding his way past the security cordon. There are tears in his eyes as he shakes everyone by the hand. Then the Championship trophy is passed to him. If anyone deserves to lay his hands on it, it is Uncle Jack. It has cost him £60m but it is a priceless moment for a man who has waited a lifetime to see his home town club win the domestic game's biggest prize. At the other end of the age scale, a young lad who has been our mascot for the day joins in the celebrations and is a focal point for the cameramen. No one knows his name but word gets around among the Press that it is Tim Flowers' son. Confusing, because to our knowledge, he has two daughters and no other kids. He has obviously been keeping quiet about this one. Our lap of honour is incredibly emotional and accompanied by the chant from both sets of fans: 'Are you watching Manchester?' The Liverpool supporters are as overjoyed as our own. Their team has beaten the new Champions, and the title has not gone to their arch-rivals from Old Trafford but to one of the legends from their own glorious past, Kenny Dalglish.

I have one more task to complete before I leave the pitch. As I came out for half-time a fan wearing a red Liverpool shirt and a blue and white Blackburn scarf leans over the tunnel area and asks me if he can have my shirt at the end. I tell him it is already spoken for but he can have my warm-up top instead and I am happy to oblige him. The shirt itself is not going anywhere. This one is for me. I shall frame it and cherish it forever.

Back in the dressing-room, the place is awash with champagne and tears of joy but the party has only just begun. Nothing has been planned in case it did not go our way but the gaffer is a friend of the proprietor of one of our favourite haunts – the Bistro French in Preston – and he arranges for us to spend the night there. Players and wives clamber aboard the coach and thousands of fans – both Blackburn and Liverpool – are still waiting to give us a send-off from Anfield.

The Drifters pop group are on live at the Bistro French and I don't think the place is quite ready for what is about to hit them. We arrive armed with bottles of bubbly which are sprayed at anyone within firing range. I look down and see one diner, who has become an instant Rovers' fan, tucking into a plate of chicken swimming in champagne. After our meal in a private room, we rejoin the main gathering to dance the night away. By the early hours the floor is deserted – everyone is up on the tables. We finally arrive home at four in the morning and I switch on the TV to check today's results on Teletext. It is reassuring to see we are still on top of the Premiership and no one can shift us now. I notice that Newcastle have finished sixth. That reminds me – I have won a bet. At the start of last season I had a wager with an uncle and a pal of my dad's that Newcastle would not finish in the top five and gave them odds of 2-1. That cost me £300 but we repeated it this season and I can look forward to pocketing £150 on my next trip to the north-east. I collapse into bed at around five o'clock and fall fast asleep – the first time for ages I can remember doing so after a game. Mind you, it did finish eleven hours ago.

MONDAY 15TH

Somewhere in the back of my mind I remember we agreed to meet up at Tim Flowers' house at midday for a drink. It seemed like a good idea at the time but this morning I am not so sure my sore head will cope. Still, we cannot let the lad down and he needs some help to polish off some extra booze he has acquired. Last Wednesday, when there were fifteen minutes left in the Manchester United-Southampton game with the score at 1-1, he sent Jane out to the off licence to buy £100 worth of drinks in readiness for an impromptu title celebration. As I have said before, it pays not to take anything for granted and Denis Irwin's penalty winner wrecked the party plans. But we can go ahead with them today and, although the first few drinks are a struggle, we soon get into the swing again.

Neil Ruddock appears to have become an honorary Blackburn player for a few days and gatecrashes our celebrations but it is good to have him around – even if it is just to remind him we are the champions.

We are due to be at the training ground at 5.15 p.m. to get the coach to Ewood Park where the Championship trophy will be formally presented to us in front of our fans. Somehow we arrange to miss that deadline. Tim, Mike Newell and Neil Ruddock and I make our own way in a convoy of four cars driven by our respective wives who have been sensible enough to stay sober. The scenes in and around Ewood Park are fantastic. The whole town seems to have turned out to see the title brought to Blackburn for the first time in 81 years.

Before the presentation we are entertained in one of the private suites and enjoy watching a Blackburn veterans team in action against the current coaching staff.

The gaffer is embarrassing. Every time he gives the ball away, which is quite often, he clutches his hamstring but the biggest laugh of the night comes when Ray Harford is hit in the face by a ball driven at him from five yards.

The trophy is handed over again and it is even more special tonight because there are over 30,000 Rovers fans to witness the event. The gaffer gets another roof-raising ovation after being presented with the Manager of the Year award and a lap of honour gives us the chance to show our appreciation to the supporters who have helped to make all this possible. By about 10.30 p.m. the party is starting to wind down and Tim is one of the first to leave. We're not far behind him but on the way home we remember that Tim still has some booze left from lunchtime. We arrange on our car phones to meet at his house in half an hour, though I suggest I had better ring him first to tell him we are on our way. 'You can forget that, I am off to bed,' he roars and slams the phone down. We finish up at Mike's house instead but we are beginning to run out of steam.

It has been a memorable few days and soon life will have to get back to normal. However, this is not the end of Blackburn's success story. It is merely the start. There are more titles and trophies to be won at home and abroad. These are no longer pipe-dreams but real targets, fuelled by the ambitions of an owner who refuses to accept second best. But any thoughts of future triumphs can wait. I want to enjoy this one first. I want to savour the pleasure of this amazing season and relive the moments when Blackburn Rovers were crowned Champions. But first I must get some sleep. I collapse into bed at 1.30 a.m. Then total, blissful oblivion . . .

P.S. I never did start the Italian lessons!

SHEARER'S YEAR

The 1994/95 season will be remembered as the time when the Beautiful Game turned ugly during the so-called season of sleaze.

It will also be remembered as the season of Shearer. If football needed an exorcist to purge itself of its demons, it found one in the Blackburn Rovers and England centre forward. If good and decent things are to triumph over evil, then this indeed was Alan Shearer's year. He would not seek to be anointed with such exalted claims. Shearer sees his role in football in simple terms, where enjoyment, professionalism, honesty and good behaviour are the keywords. They have become second nature to him because he was brought up to believe in them as a way of life. Shearer was taught to kick a football as a toddler and, at the same time, the difference between right and wrong.

These upright qualities, along with his skill, his maturity and a fierce determination to succeed, first brought him to the attention of the man who was to introduce him to the professional game. Jack Hixon, a north-east soccer scout, has become Shearer's guardian angel. He vividly remembers the impact the youngster made on him. 'I saw him first when he was twelve, playing for the Wallsend Boys Club and Newcastle City Schools teams and there was no doubt then that here was a boy with real ability,' recalls Jack. 'But there was more than just football skills. He was mature, but not in a precocious way, except of course with his talent. In this game, we see a lot of Shirley Temple-types who are a pain in the backside. They act old but are still children. Alan was not like that. He had a pride in his personal behaviour which he has maintained throughout his life.

'He also had an independence of spirit which enabled him to think and act for himself. It is true that, when I asked Alan senior if his son would be interested in having trials with Southampton, he replied, "Ask him. He is old enough to make his own mind up." Some might find that a strange response but it was typical of the way young Alan was allowed to grow up. His mum and dad would guide, direct and discipline him without imposing themselves too forcefully. They wanted to allow him to develop his own personality and handed him the responsibility of making his own decision.'

Kenny Dalglish was impressed with Shearer's appealing character when he made his initial move to sign him from Southampton for £3.3m. Dalglish's first meeting with Alan senior and his wife Anne confirmed all he needed to know. 'Our assistant manager, Ray Harford, had worked with Alan when he was in charge of the England Under 21 team at a tournament in Toulon so we knew basically what to expect from him,' says the Rovers boss. 'But when I met his mum and dad I could see how much his family had influenced him. They were modest and unassuming and genuinely appreciative of everything we were trying to do for him. I never had any doubt about Alan as a person but, if I did have, his parents would have convinced me about him because they are such nice people.'

Shearer removed himself from the family home at fifteen to join Southampton as a trainee. It was a journey from the outpost of the north-east to the south coast but he took it in his stride. He had made the long coach ride before, sometimes on his own, to attend training sessions during school holidays but now this was permanent. The professional game beckoned and Shearer, strong-willed and single-minded, was not going to be diverted from his chosen path. There was never any doubt in Jack Hixon's mind that it would lead right to the very top. 'When he left here to sign his YTS forms on July 1st, 1986, he was the best striker of his age from this area and I would say probably the rest of the country,' says Hixon. 'He was top drawer but keen to learn and improve every aspect of his game.' Shearer made his presence felt at The Dell with his razor-edged ambition but that was not the only eye-catching feature of the young Saint. Tim Flowers, now a club colleague, international team-mate and one of his closest footballing pals, was already a Southampton professional when the young centre forward arrived. 'He was always a handful in training matches against the first team and tried hard to impress the management,' says Flowers. 'But the thing that stuck in my memory at first was the way he looked. He had this bloody awful hairdo, parted at the side with a big quiff at the front. Then there were his big, heavy thighs. They were men's legs stuck on a kid's body and looked quite odd. But they gave him an advantage over the others because he was always a lot stronger than the rest.'

Shearer's anatomy had not gone unnoticed among the management hierarchy. He had the build and balance which were ideal for a striker in the modern game and Southampton's manager of the day, Chris Nicholl, recognised his physique and exploited it to the full. 'He had the same sort of physical attributes as Mark Hughes and Kenny Dalglish – big, strong legs, wide hips and a big backside. He also had the same low centre of gravity. All these things are vital to a striker because they give him the strength to take the ball with his back to goal, enable him to protect it with his body and hold off his defender until support arrives.'

The strength was there in abundance but, according to Nicholl, at first the skill was not. It took hours of painstaking individual tuition to improve his first touch but he was a willing pupil. 'Alan was a quiet lad but he was full of determination – not just to win but to improve himself,' says Nicholl. 'There was no doubt that his skills needed to be worked upon. In our youth side of that time he was the centre forward with Matthew Le Tissier and Rodney Wallace either side of him. He was definitely the late developer of the trio. Alan did not have the same flair or natural ability as the other two but, by heck, he would work hard. We used to spend hour upon hour with him in the gym, throwing and kicking hundreds and hundreds of balls at him. We taught him to hold them up, lay them off or turn to run his defender. We worked especially hard on his left side which was always his weaker flank. He loved it, kept coming back for more and eventually all the work paid off. Alan was ahead of his time and so were Matt Le Tissier and Rodney Wallace. They spent hardly any time in our reserves because they were so far advanced with their development. I had no qualms about picking any of them for the first team, especially Alan and he responded in a spectacular fashion.' The hat-trick he scored as a seventeen year old on his debut against Arsenal earner Shearer a place in the record books. He became the youngest player to notch three goals in the top flight and the youngest to accomplish the feat on his debut. Within a week, Southampton had offered him his first professional contract and Nicholl was to discover that he was as tough an opponent across the negotiating table as he was in the penalty area. Guided from long distance by Jack Hixon, Shearer spelt out his demands and refused to waver from them. Says Nicholl: 'He had no contract and we knew his hometown club Newcastle were watching the situation so we had to get these negotiations right. Alan stood his ground and, even as a seventeen year old, he knew his worth and would accept nothing less.' But somewhere along the line, Shearer's reputation for cashing in on his worth has become somewhat distorted.

He cannot step within a twenty mile radius of Old Trafford without being called a 'greedy b*****d' by Manchester United fans. This abuse started around the time of his decision to sign for Blackburn and ever since United supporters have wrongly accused him of accepting Jack Walker's bag of gold rather than United's glory. Shearer is never slow to point out that he never had the chance of signing for Alex Ferguson's team. He had an option of one – Blackburn Rovers – and he was delighted to accept it. It still hurts Jack Hixon to hear the savage taunts from United fans. 'Greed has never been part of his make-up,' he says. 'He does not have a selfish bone in his body. I agree with

Chris Nicholl, Alan knows how to assess his own value to a team and there is nothing wrong with that.' Kenny Dalglish offers another view of Shearer's earning power. He reckons the priority in the striker's life will never be money. 'He wants to be happy,' says the Rovers manager. 'Because of his background, it is important for him and his family to feel comfortable. It wouldn't mean anything to him to earn more money at another club if he was not happy being there.'

Shearer found true happiness by joining Dalglish in Blackburn, but not before he had fine-tuned his skills at Southampton – and developed the ruthless streak which all modern strikers need. Another former goalkeeping colleague from his Dell days, the nomadic veteran John Burridge, taught him one vital lesson and discovered to his painful cost that Shearer was a model pupil. 'When he was a lad at Southampton he would always want to join in any training session that was going on,' recalls Burridge. 'I used to arrange little three-a-side matches with the goals pulled in really close. Once I went down at Alan's feet to get the ball and he jumped over me. I took him to one side and told him, "Look, son, when a keeper dives at your feet, he expects you to clatter him. Don't disappoint him." ' A couple of years later Burridge was playing in a friendly for Falkirk against a Southampton team which included Shearer. Burridge says: 'I had to throw myself at Alan's feet and he followed through for the ball, caught me on the head with his boot and split my head open. I needed three stitches in the wound but I stood up, patted him on the head and said, "Well done, son. I'm proud of you." '

Tim Flowers has watched his mate develop more keenly than most and monitored his progress at Southampton and now at Blackburn. 'I never had any doubt he would make it. He was a very good player but, in those early days, his great attribute was his strength – both mental and physical. Even as a kid, he behaved like a young man. He was not a great goal-scorer for Southampton but, since moving to Blackburn, he has learned to score goals, though I suppose it helps being in a side that is striving to win things rather than fighting against relegation. He is one of the lads in a team where no one believes they are more special than anyone else. He has never been a big nightclubber or pub-goer but he likes a good laugh. He comes out with some odd sayings at times. Once when he was talking about someone he doesn't particularly like he said, "I wouldn't waste my strength by moving my eyes to look at him." He is very much a family man but he is a good mate and very loyal to his friends like Mike Newell, myself and Neil Ruddock.'

It goes without saying that his loyalty extends right back to the very start . . . to Jack Hixon. Hardly a day goes by without Shearer speaking to him. 'There is an age difference of about 50 years and people ask what can we possibly have in common,' says Hixon. 'I could never usurp his family ties but I do feel very close to him. I have a collection of England international shirts he has worn at every level. I do not have to frame them and put them on display. They are in a wardrobe at my home. They are inviolable and invaluable.

'Alan will ring me up and ask, "Any news? What's happening with Steve Davis, Tommy Widdrington and Neil Maddison?" They were all his mates at Southampton and he loves to keep track of them. He calls me from all over the world. He once rang me from the Seychelles to tell me how bloody hot it was!'

At the end of Blackburn's Championship season, Shearer is in his prime, rated universally by supporters (give or take the odd 40,000 or so Manchester United fans) and his fellow professionals. In many ways he is a throwback to a football age where players performed their heroics on the field and remained role models to young onlookers off it. Professional Footballers' Association chief executive Gordon Taylor draws a parallel between Shearer and the idols of his own boyhood. 'In days gone by we had Tom Finney who was the leader of the Preston team in every sense of the word as was Stanley Matthews at Blackpool,' says Taylor. 'Nat Lofthouse was my own particular hero and I compare Alan Shearer to him because he really does lead from the front and he puts his head in where it hurts. Where he differs from stars of the past is that he is paid a good deal more money but no one resents him that because he earns it. He is a perfect example to hold up to youngsters – like Gary Lineker in more recent years but with a bit more steel. He is a real man's man. He has become a flagship for football, not just with his performances but with his behaviour off the field. If all players behaved like Alan Shearer, my job would be a lot easier.'

Shearer's football deeds for club and country have made him one of the game's hottest properties and a road has opened up before him which could eventually bring the world's biggest clubs to his doorstep. He will follow his own chosen route, though, refusing to be rushed into snap decisions and instant judgements. There will come a time when he has to decide whether Blackburn can satisfy his search for success and happiness or whether he needs to change direction. According to Jack Hixon, the choice will be his and his alone. 'If the question ever gets around to him moving to Italy, for example, he will take advice and then analyse the situation from every angle,' says Hixon. 'Alan has a very sharp mind. He is streetwise without being nasty. He will look at the schooling for his children, the weather and the whole change of lifestyle for his family. Just as he did when he went to Southampton as a boy and to Blackburn as Britain's most expensive player of the time, he will make up his own mind and you wouldn't bet against him getting it just right, yet again. The question of him being successful doesn't come into it. People talk about him being one of Europe's best. That makes me smile. He has been world class for the last couple of years.'

Dave Harrison
May 1995

THE GOALS THAT WON THE CHAMPIONSHIP

Saturday 20th August 1994
FA Carling Premiership

Southampton 1	Blackburn Rovers 1
Banger (15)	Shearer (61)

Southampton: Grobbelaar, Kenna, Hall, Widdrington, Benali, Charlton, Allen, Magilton, Maddison, Le Tissier, Banger. Subs: Heaney, Whiston, Beasant (gk).

Blackburn: Flowers, Berg, Gale, Hendry, Le Saux, Ripley, Sherwood, Slater, Wilcox, Shearer, Sutton. Subs: Atkins, Pearce, Mimms (gk).

Attendance: 14,209 *Points*: 1 *League Position*: –

Goal 1
It is the opening game of the season and everyone is keen to do well, especially me after suffering a virus which the medical experts felt sure would keep me out of action for several games. My start to the new campaign can hardly have been worse as Bruce Grobbelaar saves my first-half penalty. I am desperate to make amends and my chance comes after half-time when Chris Sutton touches a cross from Graeme Le Saux on to me. There are claims from the Saints' defenders that I handled the ball as I brought it under control but I never touched it. I sweep it under Grobbelaar's body and I am off the mark for the season –

always a satisfying feeling. There is even more attention focused on us than usual because this is the first time the £8 million-plus Sutton-Shearer partnership has been seen. We feel we have performed reasonably well as a pair when you consider we have not had much time to develop an understanding.

Tuesday 23rd August 1994
FA Carling Premiership

Blackburn Rovers 3 Leicester City 0

Sutton (18)
Berg (59)
Shearer (73)

Blackburn: Flowers, Berg, Gale, Hendry, Le Saux, Ripley, Sherwood, Slater, Wilcox, Shearer, Sutton. Subs: Warhurst, Pearce, Mimms (gk).

Leicester: Ward, Grayson, Willis, Hill, Mohan, Whitlow, Agnew, Blake, Draper, Joachim, Walsh. Subs: Thompson, Roberts, Poole (gk).

Attendance: 21,050 *Points*: 4 *League Position*: –

Goal 2
Just as I was determined to score on the opening day, I consider it just as important to mark my first appearance of the new campaign at home with a goal. We are already well in control when Robbie Slater runs through with only the goalkeeper to beat. His shot hits the post and comes back to me barely a yard from goal. Goals do not come much easier than this tap-in but I'll take anything that's offered on a plate. They all look good on the scoresheet, whether they're simple or spectacular. I am pleased with my overall performance today and most of the newspapers and football magazines award me nine out of ten. There are more encouraging signs from the partnership with Chris Sutton

when he scores his first goal for Blackburn, assisted by yours truly.

Saturday 27th August 1994
FA Carling Premiership

Blackburn Rovers 4 Coventry City 0

Sutton (67, 74, 88)
Wilcox (77)

Blackburn: Flowers, Warhurst, Gale, Hendry, Le Saux, Ripley, Sherwood, Slater, Wilcox, Shearer, Sutton. Subs: Pearce, Atkins, Mimms (gk).

Coventry: Ogrizovic, Borrows, Morgan, Darby, Rennie, Babb, Flynn, Wegerle, Quinn, Cook, Busst. Subs: Boland, Williams, Gould (gk).

Attendance: 21,657 *Points*: 7 *League Position*: 2nd

Wednesday 31st August 1994
FA Carling Premiership

Arsenal 0 Blackburn Rovers 0

Arsenal: Seaman, Dixon, Keown, Adams, Winterburn, Jensen, Schwarz, Campbell, Merson, Wright, Smith. Subs: Linighan, Dickov, Bartram (gk).

Blackburn: Flowers, Berg, Gale, Hendry, Le Saux, Ripley, Slater, Sherwood, Wilcox, Shearer, Sutton. Subs: Marker, Warhurst, Mimms (gk).

Attendance: 37,629 *Points*: 8 *League Position*: 7th

Saturday 10th September 1994
FA Carling Premiership

Blackburn Rovers 3 Everton 0

Shearer (17, pen 60)
Wilcox (43)

Blackburn: Flowers, Berg, Gale, Hendry, Le Saux, Ripley, Sherwood, Slater, Wilcox, Shearer, Sutton. Subs: Atkins, Pearce, Mimms (gk).

Everton: Southall, Jackson, Watson, Unsworth, Burrows, Stuart, Samways, Ebbrell, Limpar, Amokachi, Rideout. Subs: Hinchcliffe, Angell, Keaton (gk).

Attendance: 26,538 *Points*: 11 *League Position*: 3rd

Goals 3 and 4
The value of getting the ball forward quickly is emphasised by my first goal today. Tim Flowers hits a long clearance my way and I hold off David Unsworth, turn him and shoot past Neville Southall from about 25 yards. Looking back, it is one of my best strikes of the season. I am delighted with my second goal from the penalty spot because it had been agreed before the game I should continue taking them despite my miss against Southampton. I learn from my mistake at The Dell, when I changed my mind about where I was going to put it. This time I place my shot firmly and decisively past Neville, who goes the wrong way. The big Everton keeper gets his own back later in the second half by denying me a hat-trick.

Tuesday 13th September 1994
UEFA Cup First Round, First Leg

Blackburn Rovers 0 Trelleborg 1

Sandell (71)

Blackburn: Flowers, Berg, Gale, Hendry, Le Saux, Ripley, Sherwood, Slater, Wilcox, Shearer, Sutton. Subs: Atkins, Makel Pearce, Wright, Mimms (gk).

Trelleborg: Jankowski, Mattson, C. Karlsson, Brorsson, M. Andersson, Hansson, Severin, Engqvist, Blixt, J. Karlsson, Sandell. Subs: Larsson, Eriksson, Neilsson, Persson, A. Andersson (gk).

Attendance: 13,755

Sunday 18th September 1994
FA Carling Premiership

Chelsea 1 | Blackburn Rovers 2

Spencer (56) | Johnsen (og 26), Sutton (65)

Chelsea: Kharine, Clarke, Kjeldbjerg, Johnsen, Sinclair, Wise, Peacock, Spackman, Rocastle, Furlong, Spencer. Subs: Newton, Fleck, Colgan (gk).

Blackburn: Flowers, Berg, Gale, Hendry, Le Saux, Ripley, Sherwood, Atkins, Slater, Shearer, Sutton. Subs: Warhurst, Pearce, Mimms (gk).

Attendance: 17,513 *Points*: 14 *League Position*: 2nd

Tuesday 20th September 1994
Coca-Cola Cup Second Round, First Leg

Blackburn Rovers 2 | Birmingham City 0

Wilcox (55)
Sutton (68)

Blackburn: Flowers, Berg, Warhurst, Hendry, Le Saux, Ripley, Sherwood, Atkins, Slater, Wilcox, Sutton. Subs: Makel, Pearce, Mimms (gk).

Birmingham: Bennett, Scott, Frain, Ward, Dryden, Whyte, Harding, Claridge, Cooper, Tait, Wallace. Subs: Dominguez, McGavin, Price (gk).

Attendance: 14,517

Saturday 24th September 1994
FA Carling Premiership

Blackburn Rovers 3	Aston Villa 1
Shearer (pen 17, 72) Sutton (56)	Ehiogu (90)

Blackburn: Flowers, Berg, Gale, Hendry, Le Saux, Ripley, Sherwood, Atkins, Wilcox, Shearer, Sutton. Subs: Warhurst, Pearce, Mimms (gk).

Villa: Bosnich, Barrett, Teale, McGrath, Ehiogu, Staunton, Yorke, Richardson, Townsend, Saunders, Atkinson. Subs: Lamptey, Fenton, Spink (gk).

Attendance: 22,694 *Points*: 17 *League Position*: 2nd

Goals 5 and 6
Yet another penalty enables me to open the scoring against Villa and there is extra pressure on me because their goalkeeper Mark Bosnich is developing a reputation for saving them. My confidence is high after converting the one against Everton and Bosnich dives the opposite way to where I place my shot. We are able to build on this lead and produce a terrific team performance. Chris Sutton adds a second and I score again with a goal which the so-called purists would describe as a typical route one effort. Chris and myself both run through on to Tim Flowers' long kick and my partner nods it down for me to take a touch and thump it past Bosnich. OK, so it might not be the most creative way to score a goal but when you have two strikers

full of energy and hungry for goals, there is not much a defence can do to stop it. The Sutton and Shearer strike force looks devastating today, sharing the three goals between us and causing Villa endless problems.

Tuesday 27th September 1994
UEFA Cup First Round, Second Leg

Trelleborg 2	Blackburn Rovers 2
J. Karlsson (49, 85)	Sutton (10) Shearer (83)

Trelleborg: Jankowski, Brorsson, C. Karlsson, M. Andersson, Mattsson, Palmer, Engqvist, Severin, Hansson, J. Karlsson, Sandell. Subs: Larsson, Eriksson, Neilsson, Blixt, A. Andersson (gk).

Blackburn: Flowers, Berg, Gale, Hendry, Le Saux, Ripley, Sherwood, Atkins, Wilcox, Shearer, Sutton. Subs: Warhurst, Pearce, Slater, Morrison, Mimms (gk).

Attendance: 6,730

Goal 7
We discovered during the first leg that Trelleborg are a good side, certainly not the bunch of Swedish no-hopers depicted by the Press, but we are confident we can repair the damage caused at Ewood Park. We need an early away goal to peg back their advantage from the first game and manage to get that through Chris Sutton. When I score a second to put us 2-1 up with a close-range header after Ian Pearce heads a corner back towards me, we think we have done enough to take us through. Then bang, they go straight to the other end and equalise and we are out of Europe at the first hurdle. We are hammered by the media for losing to a team of part-timers but Trelleborg are no mugs and they go on to give another good account of themselves in the next round, losing by the only goal in the last minute against Lazio.

Saturday 1st October 1994
FA Carling Premiership

Norwich City 2 Blackburn Rovers 1

Bowen (30) Sutton (4)
Newsome (55)

Norwich: Gunn, Bradshaw, Newsome, Polston, Bowen, Adams, Crook, Milligan, Eadie, Newman, Ekoku. Subs: Goss, Robins, Marshall (gk).

Blackburn: Flowers, Warhurst, Berg, Hendry, Le Saux, Ripley, Sherwood, Atkins, Wilcox, Shearer, Sutton. Subs: Slater, Pearce, Mimms (gk).

Attendance: 18,146 *Points*: 17 *League Position*: 3rd

Tuesday 4th October 1994
Coca-Cola Cup Second Round, Second Leg

Birmingham City 1 Blackburn Rovers 1 (Agg 1-3)

McGavin (9) Sutton (71)

Birmingham: Bennett, Bass, Frain, Ward, Daish, Barnett, De Souza, Shearer, McGavin, Dominguez, Donowa. Subs: Wallace, Moulden, Price (gk).

Blackburn: Flowers, Warhurst, Berg, Hendry, Le Saux, Ripley, Sherwood, Atkins, Wilcox, Shearer, Sutton. Subs: Morrison, Pearce, Mimms (gk)

Attendance: 16,275

Sunday 9th October 1994
FA Carling Premiership

Newcastle United 1	Blackburn Rovers 1
Flowers (og 88)	Shearer (pen 59)

Newcastle: Srnicek, Hottiger, Howey, Peacock, Beresford, Fox, Watson, Lee, Sellars, Beardsley, Cole. Subs: Clark, Kitson, Hooper (gk).

Blackburn: Flowers, Berg, Hendry, Warhurst, Le Saux, Ripley, Sherwood, Atkins, Wilcox, Shearer, Sutton. Subs: Slater, Pearce, Mimms (gk).

Attendance: 34,344 *Points*: 18 *League Position*: 3rd

Goal 8
My family and several friends are at St James's Park, so I am really fired up to do well against my hometown team. I was a fanatical Newcastle fan as a boy and hated to see them lose but now it gives me an enormous amount of pleasure to score against them. My goal comes from yet another penalty, awarded after Jason Wilcox is brought down by Pavel Srnicek. There is a long delay while Jason receives treatment and that builds up the pressure on me. It is at the Gallowgate End where I used to stand with the Toon Army as a lad and I take some stick from the home fans as I wait to take the penalty. I would have preferred to place the ball down and stick it away immediately but I manage to keep my nerve and once more the keeper goes the wrong way. My spot-kick total is building up nicely after that first day miss. Some people argue that penalty goals are not worth as much as those scored in open play but to me goals are goals. They still have to be put away and the pressure is always on the penalty taker, whereas the keeper has everything to gain and nothing to lose.

Saturday 15th October 1994
FA Carling Premiership

Blackburn Rovers 3	Liverpool 2
Atkins (52)	Fowler (29)
Sutton (57, 77)	Barnes (59)

Blackburn: Flowers, Berg, Gale, Hendry, Le Saux, Ripley, Atkins, Warhurst, Wilcox, Shearer, Sutton. Subs: Slater, Pearce, Mimms (gk).

Liverpool: James, Scales, Ruddock, Babb, Jones, Barnes, McManaman, Molby, Bjornebye, Rush, Fowler. Subs: Clough, Redknapp, Stensgaard (gk).

Attendance: 30,263 *Points*: 21 *League Position*: 3rd

Sunday 23rd October 1994
FA Carling Premiership

Blackburn Rovers 2	Manchester United 4
Warhurst (13)	Cantona (pen 45)
Hendry (51)	Kanchelskis (52, 82)
	Hughes (67)

Blackburn: Flowers, Berg, Gale, Hendry, Le Saux, Ripley, Atkins, Warhurst, Wilcox, Shearer, Sutton. Subs: Slater, Pearce, Mimms (gk).

Manchester United: Schmeichel, Keane, Bruce, Pallister, Irwin, Kanchelskis, Butt, Ince, Sharpe, Cantona, Hughes. Subs: McClair, Gillespie, Walsh (gk).

Attendance: 30,260 *Points*: 21 *League Position*: 4th

Wednesday 26th October 1994
Coca-Cola Cup Third Round

Blackburn Rovers 2 | Coventry City 0

Shearer (54, 63)

Blackburn: Flowers, Berg, Gale, Hendry, Le Saux, Ripley, Atkins, Warhurst, Wilcox, Shearer, Sutton. Subs: Pearce, Makel, Mimms (gk).

Coventry: Ogrizovic, Pickering, Busst, Rennie, Borrows, Flynn, Darby, Cook, Ndlovu, Dublin, Wegerle. Subs: Jones, Williams, Gould (gk).

Attendance: 14,538

Goals 9 and 10
After the controversial defeat against our main rivals Manchester United, it is imperative we bounce straight back. Two goals against Coventry in the Coca-Cola Cup help remove some of the bitter taste left behind by Sunday's defeat but the atmosphere at the game is very flat. My first comes from Stuart Ripley's cross from the right which finds me five or six yards from goal. I escape the attention of my marker and get my head to the ball. There is no need to generate any real power from this range. It was just a case of making sure I hit the target and I did. I reach double figures for the season with a shot from fifteen yards. I swivel on to a cross from Jason Wilcox on the left and make contact with my right foot. The ball flies into the net through a crowd of players and we are in the next round.

Saturday 29th October 1994
FA Carling Premiership

Nottingham Forest 0 | Blackburn Rovers 2

Sutton (7, 68)

Forest: Crossley, Little, Cooper, Chettle, Pearce, Stone, Bohinen, Phillips, Woan, Roy, Lee. Subs: Haaland, Wright, Black (gk).

Blackburn: Flowers, Berg, Hendry, Warhurst, Le Saux, Ripley, Sherwood, Atkins, Wilcox, Sutton, Shearer. Subs: Gale, Pearce, Mimms (gk).

Attendance: 22,131 *Points*: 24 *League Position*: 4th

Wednesday 2nd November 1994
FA Carling Premiership

Sheffield Wednesday 0 Blackburn Rovers 1

Shearer (53)

Sheffield Wednesday: Pressman, Atherton, Walker, Pearce, Nolan, Taylor, Sheridan, Hyde, Sinton, Bart-Williams, Bright. Subs: Petrescu, Watson, Key (gk).

Blackburn: Flowers, Berg, Hendry, Gale, Le Saux, Ripley, Sherwood, Warhurst, Wilcox, Shearer, Sutton. Subs: Newell, Atkins, Mimms (gk).

Attendance: 24,297 *Points*: 27 *League Position*: 2nd

Goal 11
A one-two out on the left with Jason Wilcox leaves me to take the ball in my stride and I manage to scoop the ball into the net with my right foot as it bends away. The goal comes at the end at Hillsborough where the Rovers fans are gathered and they leap to their feet. We always try to kick towards our own supporters in the second half because their vocal backing can give us an extra lift as the game wears on and our legs become tired. My goal earns us the three points and lifts us back into second place behind Newcastle. Already some pundits are beginning to write about us as potential champions and we have only just entered November.

Saturday 5th November 1994
FA Carling Premiership

Blackburn Rovers 2 | Tottenham Hotspur 0

Wilcox (8)
Shearer (pen 49)

Blackburn: Flowers, Berg, Hendry, Gale, Le Saux, Ripley, Sherwood, Warhurst, Wilcox, Shearer, Sutton. Subs: Newell, Atkins, Mimms (gk).

Spurs: Walker, Kerslake, Mabbutt, Popescu, Campbell, Edinburgh, Dozzell, Howells, Barmby, Sheringham, Klinsmann. Subs: Hazzard, Rosenthal, Day (gk).

Attendance: 26,933 *Points*: 30 *League Position*: 2nd

Goal 12
I almost score inside the opening ten minutes but my shot hits the inside of the post. Thankfully Jason Wilcox is following up to push home the rebound. I am again on target from the penalty spot after Justin Edinburgh brings me down as I surge into the box. Ian Walker guesses right and gets both his hands to the ball. Perhaps he should have saved it but there is enough power on the shot to force it into the net. It's a big relief to see it go in because when a keeper goes the right way he gives himself a really good chance of stopping the ball.

Saturday 19th November 1994
FA Carling Premiership

Ipswich Town 1 | Blackburn Rovers 3

Thomson (18)

Sutton (8)
Sherwood (40)
Shearer (70)

Ipswich: Forrest, Yallop, Linighan, Youds, Whelan, Thomson, Mason, Williams, Sedgley, Marshall, Paz. Subs: Geuntchev, Milton, Morgan (gk).

Blackburn: Flowers, Warhurst, Gale, Pearce, Le Saux, Ripley, Sherwood, Atkins, Slater, Shearer, Sutton. Subs: Newell, Wright, Mimms (gk).

Attendance: 17,329 *Points*: 33 *League Position*: 2nd

Goal 13
I do not have to work too hard for my goal today. Chris Sutton has a fierce header saved by Craig Forrest and I am left with a tap-in from two yards. They look easy but there is a knack to being in the right place at the right time and this is a perfect example of that. The partnership between Chris and myself is looking stronger and stronger at this stage of the season. We are not just scoring goals, but we are providing chances for each other. We are also managing to carry the burden of having big price tags around our necks, though I dare say the vultures are hovering in case we stop producing. Fortunately neither of us has hit a lean spell in front of goal yet. We are both hard-working strikers and if you keep grafting away, there is a fair chance that opportunities will come along.

Saturday 26th November 1994
FA Carling Premiership

Blackburn Rovers 4 Queens Park Rangers 0

Sutton (9)
Shearer (56, pen 66, 85)

Blackburn: Flowers, Warhurst, Pearce, Berg, Le Saux, Ripley, Sherwood, Atkins, Slater, Shearer, Sutton. Subs: Newell, Wright, Mimms (gk).

QPR: Dykstra, Yates, Ready, McDonald, Wilson, Impey, Barker, Hodge, Sinclair, Ferdinand, Gallen. Subs: Holloway, Brevett, Roberts (gk).

Attendance: 21,302 *Points*: 36 *League Position*: 1st

Goals 14, 15 and 16
All three of my goals come in the second half at the end where most of the home fans are gathered. Chris Sutton again plays a big part in the first, flicking on a free-kick for me to score. I am pulled back by Karl Ready but rather than wait for a penalty award, I am strong enough to shrug him off and fire the ball through the keeper's legs. Goal number two comes from the penalty spot after Stuart Ripley fools Ready with a superb turn and is pulled down by the Rangers defender. The third probably stakes a claim to be my best goal of the season. There are a few minutes left when I collect a nod-down from substitute Mike Newell and since we are comfortably ahead I decide to try a shot. If I had been that far out in the opening five minutes I would almost certainly have passed. But with two goals in the bag and the points already won, I go for it . . . and the ball flies into the net off the underside of the bar. People often expect me to be more excited when I score a great goal, especially when it completes a hat-trick, but you will never find me doing handstands, back flips or laps of honour. The most you'll get out of me is a punch in the air. I do feel on top of the world tonight, however, because this is my first hat-trick of the season and we have taken over the leadership of the Premiership.

Wednesday 30th November 1994
Coca-Cola Cup Fourth Round

Blackburn Rovers 1	Liverpool 3
Sutton (89)	Rush (19, 51, 73)

Blackburn: Flowers, Berg, Gale, Hendry, Warhurst, Le Saux, Ripley, Sherwood, Wilcox, Shearer, Sutton. Subs: Newell, Atkins, Mimms (gk).

Liverpool: James, R. Jones, Babb, Rush, Scales, Redknapp, Thomas, McManaman, Bjornebye, Fowler, Ruddock. Subs: Clough, L. Jones, Warner (gk).

Attendance: 30,115

Saturday 3rd December 1994
FA Carling Premiership

Wimbledon 0 Blackburn Rovers 3

Atkins (52)
Wilcox (72)
Shearer (74)

Wimbledon: Segers, Cunningham, Fitzgerald, Thorn, Elkins, Fear, Barton, Leonhardson, Clarke, Holdsworth, Ekoku. Subs: Harford, Ardley, Sullivan (gk).

Blackburn: Flowers, Warhurst, Berg, Hendry, Le Saux, Ripley, Sherwood, Atkins, Wilcox, Shearer, Sutton. Subs: Newell, Pearce, Mimms (gk).

Attendance: 12,341 *Points*: 39 *League Position*: 1st

Goal 17
We are two goals up through Mark Atkins and Jason Wilcox and the game is well under our control. But you will never find me relaxing for a minute, especially if my name is not on the scoresheet. Scoring goals is the greatest feeling in the world and I want to experience it as often as I can. I am never satisfied even when we are cruising to victory. Chris Sutton breaks clear, squares the ball to me and I take a touch before sliding it past

Hans Segers. I feel the same pleasure as if it had been the winner in a closely-fought encounter.

Saturday 10th December 1994
FA Carling Premiership

Blackburn Rovers 3	Southampton 2
Atkins (6) Shearer (13, 74)	Le Tissier (65, 78)

Blackburn: Flowers, Warhurst, Hendry, Berg, Le Saux, Ripley, Sherwood, Atkins, Wilcox, Shearer, Sutton. Subs: Newell, Slater, Mimms (gk).

Southampton: Grobbelaar, Kenna, Hall, Monkou, Benali, Charlton, Widdrington, Maddison, Magilton, Le Tissier, Ekelund. Subs: Maskell, Hughes, Beasant (gk).

Attendance: 23,372 *Points*: 42 *League Position*: 1st

Goals 18 and 19
We are already a goal up from an early Mark Atkins strike when Richard Hall gives me a tug in the penalty area. Referee Alan Wilkie sees it and awards a spot-kick. That leaves me in a dilemma. Bruce Grobbelaar saved my penalty on the opening day of the season, so do I go for the opposite corner this time or is that too obvious? Shall I try to double bluff Bruce and go for the same side? In the end I opt for the other side but he outguesses me again. Fortunately, the ball comes straight out to me and I am able to net the rebound from five yards. What a relief. My second goal is a timely one because Matthew Le Tissier is threatening to bring Southampton back into the match with some inspirational stuff. Graeme Le Saux goes down the left, Mark Atkins dummies his low cross and, after controlling it, I chip the ball over Grobbelaar into the roof of the net.

Saturday 17th December 1994
FA Carling Premiership

Leicester City 0 Blackburn Rovers 0

Leicester: Poole, Grayson, Hill, Willis, Whitlow, Blake, Draper, Thompson, Philpott, Gee, Oldfield. Subs: Joachim, Agnew, Ward (gk).

Blackburn: Flowers, Berg, Gale, Pearce, Le Saux, Ripley, Sherwood, Atkins, Wilcox, Shearer, Sutton. Subs: Newell, Slater, Mimms (gk).

Attendance: 20,559 *Points*: 43 *League Position*: 1st

Monday 26th December 1994
FA Carling Premiership

Manchester City 1 Blackburn Rovers 3

Quinn (22)

Shearer (9)
Atkins (16)
Le Saux (67)

Manchester City: Dibble, Foster, Brightwell, Kernaghan, Lomas, Summerbee, Gaudino, Flitcroft, Beagrie, Quinn, Rosler. Subs: Phelan, Vonk, Margetson (gk)

Blackburn: Flowers, Berg, Gale, Hendry, Le Saux, Ripley, Sherwood, Atkins, Wilcox, Shearer, Sutton. Subs: Newell, Warhurst, Mimms (gk).

Attendance: 23,397 *Points*: 46 *League Position*: 1st

Goal 20
This is another scrambled effort but I am quite content to chalk up my 20th of the season by whatever method available. A cross comes in from my regular supplier Graeme Le Saux and Chris

Sutton heads the ball against the crossbar. As it falls among a crowd of players in the box, I manage to get a toe end to it and force it past Andy Dibble. Some would say this is lucky but I would argue I am more determined than most to scrap for the ball once the goal is in my sights. It is a habit I hope I will never lose and I can think of no better way to celebrate Christmas than by sticking the ball in the net, particularly as it helps secure the win which keeps us on top.

Saturday 31 December 1994
FA Carling Premiership

Crystal Palace 0 | Blackburn Rovers 1

Sherwood (66)

Crystal Palace: Martyn, Humphrey, Shaw, Patterson, Coleman, Gordon, Southgate, Newman, Williams, Preece, Armstrong. Subs: Pitcher, Ndah, Wilmot (gk).

Blackburn: Flowers, Berg, Hendry, Pearce, Le Saux, Ripley, Sherwood, Atkins, Wilcox, Shearer, Sutton. Subs: Newell, Warhurst, Mimms (gk).

Attendance: 14,232 *Points*: 49 *League Position*: 1st

Monday 2nd January 1995
FA Carling Premiership

Blackburn Rovers 4 | West Ham United 2

Shearer (pen 14, 75, pen 79)
Le Saux (61)

Cottee (33)
Dicks (58)

Blackburn: Flowers, Berg, Hendry, Gale, Le Saux, Ripley, Sherwood, Atkins, Wilcox, Shearer, Sutton. Subs: Newell, Warhurst, Mimms (gk).

West Ham: Miklosko, Breacker, Potts, Rieper, Dicks, Hughes, Bishop, Moncur, Holmes, Boere, Cottee. Subs: Rush, Brown, Sealey (gk).

Attendance: 25,503 *Points*: 52 *League Position*: 1st

Goals 21, 22 and 23
Sometimes you feel lousy and the last thing you want to do is to push yourself through 90 minutes of football. This is one of those days. I am suffering from a stomach bug and it is a real effort to keep my 100 per cent appearance record for League games. It is amazing what a goal can cure. My first is from the penalty spot. There is no argument about this one because I am through and Ludo Miklosko brings me down. He dives the right way but I manage to keep the shot out of his reach. Goal number two originates from a through ball from Jason Wilcox. I just manage to stretch to control it and blast it into the corner of the net. This is a vital goal for us because West Ham are giving us a bit of a fright and have taken a 2-1 lead. I seal my hat-trick with another penalty, awarded this time for a foul by Marc Rieper on Jason Wilcox. This time Miklosko goes the wrong way and it gives me another autographed match ball for the trophy cabinet.

Sunday 8th January 1995
FA Cup Third Round

Newcastle United 1	Blackburn Rovers 1
Lee (56)	Sutton (30)

Newcastle: Srnicek, Venison, Beresford, Bracewell, Fox, Howey, Lee, Beardsley, Cole, Peacock, Elliott. Subs: Watson, Kitson, Hooper (gk).

Blackburn: Flowers, Berg, Hendry, Warhurst, Le Saux, Sherwood, Ripley, Atkins, Wilcox, Shearer, Sutton. Subs: Newell, Pearce, Mimms (gk).

Attendance: 31,721

Saturday 14th January 1995
FA Carling Premiership

Blackburn Rovers 3 — Nottingham Forest 0

Warhurst (54)
Wilcox (78)
Chettle (og 88)

Blackburn: Flowers, Berg, Hendry, Pearce, Wright, Slater, Atkins, Warhurst, Wilcox, Shearer, Sutton. Subs: Newell, Gale, Mimms (gk).

Forest: Crossley, Lyttle, Chettle, Tyler, Haaland, Stone, Gemmill, Phillips, Woan, Roy, Collymore. Subs: Webb, McGregor, Filan (gk).

Attendance: 27,510 *Points*: 55 *League Position*: 1st

Wednesday 18th January 1995
FA Cup Third Round Replay

Blackburn Rovers 1 — Newcastle United 2

Sutton (74) — Hottiger (51), Clark (88)

Blackburn: Flowers, Berg, Hendry, Pearce, Le Saux, Slater, Atkins, Warhurst, Wilcox, Shearer, Sutton. Subs: Newell, Wright, Mimms (gk).

Newcastle: Srnicek, Venison, Beresford, Hottiger, Peacock,

Howey, Lee, Fox, Elliott, Clark, Kitson. Subs: Bracewell, Watson, Hooper (gk).

Attendance: 22,658

Saturday 21st January 1995
FA Carling Premiership

Manchester United 1 Blackburn Rovers 0

Cantona (81)

Manchester United: Schmeichel, Keane, Bruce, Pallister, Irwin, Giggs, Ince, McClair, Sharpe, Cantona, Cole. Subs: May, Kanchelskis, Walsh (gk).

Blackburn: Flowers, Berg, Warhurst, Hendry, Le Saux, Wilcox, Sherwood, Atkins, Wright, Shearer, Sutton. Subs: Newell, Pearce, Mimms (gk).

Attendance: 42,742 *Points*: 55 *League Position*: 1st

Saturday 28th January 1995
FA Carling Premiership

Blackburn Rovers 4 Ipswich Town 1

Shearer (3, 29, pen 90) Wark (pen 76)
Sherwood (49)

Blackburn: Flowers, Berg, Pearce, Hendry, Le Saux, Slater, Warhurst, Sherwood, Wilcox, Shearer, Sutton. Subs: Newell, Atkins, Mimms (gk).

Ipswich: Forrest, Yallop, Wark, Whelan, Vaughan, Tanner, Sedgley, Williams, Thomson, Slater, Chapman. Subs: Johnson, Paz, Baker (gk).

Attendance: 21,325 *Points*: 58 *League Position*: 1st

Goals 24, 25 and 26
Four games without a goal demands drastic action. This has been my leanest spell of the season so I have thrown my match boots into the bin and am trying out a new pair. They work wonders. I give us an early lead by robbing Phil Whelan out on the right and blast the ball into the far corner of the net past Craig Forrest. For my second, Graeme Le Saux knocks a long ball forward and I call for Chris Sutton to flick it on with his head. I manage to cut in from the left and bang it into the top corner. These new boots are impressive. They can certainly have another outing next match. The goal which completes my hat-trick comes from the last kick of the match from the penalty spot. I am brought down by Whelan on a muddy pitch which has proved troublesome for defenders. Forrest dives the wrong way and I continue my good run of spot-kicks. I am into a good groove now. The vital thing is to stick with your decision. Any change of mind can prove disastrous because if you hesitate at the vital moment of contact, you give the keeper a greater chance of making a save.

Wednesday 1st February 1995
FA Carling Premiership

Blackburn Rovers 1 — Leeds United 1

Shearer (pen 6) — McAllister (pen 85)

Blackburn: Flowers, Berg, Hendry, Pearce, Le Saux, Atkins, Sherwood, Warhurst, Wilcox, Shearer, Sutton. Subs: Newell, Wright, Mimms (gk).

Leeds: Lukic, Kelly, Palmer, Pemberton, Dorigo, White, McAllister, Radebe, Speed, Massinga, Deane. Subs: Worthington, Yeboah, Beeney (gk).

Attendance: 28,561 *Points*: 59 *League Position*: 1st

Goal 27

Tim Flowers is sent off after two minutes for bringing down Brian Deane, so we are up against it in a big way. The statistics will show that I earn a vital point with my 27th goal of the season but in reality this is a team effort in the face of real adversity. I am left to play alone up front after Chris Sutton drops back to play centre half. It is a battle from start to finish and we are thankful to be ahead from the penalty spot after Chris is brought down. I perform my now-familiar task of sending goalkeeper John Lukic the wrong way. I don't know whether John remembers it or not but he saved the only penalty I ever took for Southampton. Maybe his memory is not as good as mine because I hit this one the same way and he dives in the opposite direction. Leeds equalise from a Gary McAllister penalty in a frenzied end to the game – we have not worked harder in any match.

Sunday 5th February 1995
FA Carling Premiership

Tottenham Hotspur 3	Blackburn Rovers 1
Klinsmann (18)	Sherwood (47)
Anderton (30)	
Barmby (80)	

Spurs: Walker, Campbell, Mabbutt, Calderwood, Edinburgh, Anderton, Popescu, Howells, Barmby, Klinsmann, Sheringham. Subs: Nethercote, Caskey, Day (gk).

Blackburn: Flowers, Berg, Hendry, Pearce, Wright, Ripley, Sherwood, Warhurst, Wilcox, Shearer, Sutton. Subs: Newell, Atkins, Given (gk).

Attendance: 28,124 *Points*: 59 *League Position*: 1st

Sunday 12th February 1995
FA Carling Premiership

Blackburn Rovers 3	Sheffield Wednesday 1
Sherwood (26)	Waddle (32)
Atkins (35)	
Shearer (66)	

Blackburn: Mimms, Berg, Pearce, Hendry, Wright, Slater, Sherwood, Atkins, Warhurst, Shearer, Sutton. Subs: Gale, Newell, Given (gk).

Sheffield Wednesday: Pressman, Atherton, Pearce, Walker, Nolan, Petrescu, Sheridan, Bart-Williams, Sinton, Waddle, Bright. Subs: Whittingham, Williams, Woods (gk).

Attendance: 22,223 *Points*: 62 *League Position*: 1st

Goal 28
On a miserable afternoon when the rain is tumbling down in bucketloads, we pocket maximum points to make our Championship prospects a lot more favourable. I manage to score the goal which puts the game out of Wednesday's reach with a header. Henning Berg's cross from the right reaches me and I head it back in the direction from which it comes. Chris Woods, on as substitute goalkeeper after Kevin Pressman is sent off for handling the ball outside his area, is beaten by the pace of the ball as it skids past him on the wet grass. I meet up with the England squad later and it is always good to report for international duty with a goal under your belt.

Wednesday 22nd February 1995
FA Carling Premiership

Blackburn Rovers 2	Wimbledon 1
Shearer (3)	Ekoku (39)
Atkins (25)	

Blackburn: Mimms, Berg, Hendry, Pearce, Le Saux, Slater, Sherwood, Atkins, Warhurst, Shearer, Newell. Subs: Wright, Ripley, Given (gk).

Wimbledon: Segers, Cunningham, Reeves, Perry, Kimble, Barton, Earle, Leonhardsen, Ardley, Ekoku, Clarke. Subs: Holdsworth, Harford, Sullivan (gk).

Attendance: 20,586 *Points*: 65 *League Position*: 1st

Goal 29
With Chris Sutton suspended, Mike Newell is my strike partner and it brings back memories of my early days at Rovers when he played such a vital role in helping me to settle in. My goal is a replica of the one I scored in the last game against Sheffield Wednesday. Henning Berg again provides the cross and my downward header gathers pace off the wet pitch to give Hans Segers very little chance. I almost grab a second towards the end but am denied by the upright. We are grateful for three points from an unspectacular performance.

Saturday 25th February 1995
FA Carling Premiership

Blackburn Rovers 0 Norwich City 0

Blackburn: Flowers, Berg, Hendry, Pearce, Le Saux, Ripley, Sherwood, Atkins, Wilcox, Shearer, Newell. Subs: Wright, Warhurst, Mimms (gk).

Norwich: Marshall, Bradshaw, Polston, Newsome, Bowen, Adams, Milligan, Johnson, Eadie, Sheron, Ward. Subs: Such, Cureton, Tracey (gk).

Attendance: 25,597 *Points*: 66 *League Position*: 1st

Saturday 4th March 1995
FA Carling Premiership

Aston Villa 0 | Blackburn Rovers 1

Hendry (12)

Villa: Bosnich, Charles, McGrath, Ehiogu, Teale, Yorke, Taylor, Townsend, Staunton, Saunders, Johnson. Subs: Fenton, Houghton, Spink (gk).

Blackburn: Flowers, Berg, Hendry, Pearce, Le Saux, Ripley, Sherwood, Atkins, Wilcox, Shearer, Sutton. Subs: Newell, Warhurst, Mimms (gk).

Attendance: 40,114 *Points*: 69 *League Position*: 1st

Wednesday 8th March 1995
FA Carling Premiership

Blackburn Rovers 3 | Arsenal 1

Shearer (4, pen 48) | Morrow (49)
Le Saux (18)

Blackburn: Flowers, Berg, Hendry, Pearce, Le Saux, Ripley, Sherwood, Atkins, Wilcox, Shearer, Sutton. Subs: Newell, Warhurst, Mimms (gk).

Arsenal: Bartram, Dixon, Linighan, Adams, Winterburn, Parlour, Schwarz, Morrow, Merson, Helder, Hartson. Subs: Wright, Bould, Harper (gk).

Attendance: 23,452 *Points*: 72 *League Position*: 1st

Goals 30 and 31
Every game, every point, every goal is crucial now as the title race enters the critical stage. I have an injection before the game because the knee injury which kept me out of the England game

against Uruguay is still causing me problems. We have been temporarily deposed as League leaders by Manchester United and need an early goal to settle us down. It comes after four minutes as I hit a firm drive from Chris Sutton's pass through Vince Bartram's legs. Graeme Le Saux puts us two up and then we get a penalty a few minutes into the second half when Mark Atkins is brought down by Andy Linighan. I have taken so many penalties this season, all of them shown on Sky, that I am sure goalkeepers have studied my technique in detail. I try to vary the direction of my spot-kicks but always stick to my golden rule – once I have made my mind up I never change it. Vince Bartram goes the wrong way, so I win this battle of wits.

Saturday 11 March 1995
FA Carling Premiership

Coventry City 1	Blackburn Rovers 1
Dublin (31)	Shearer (87)

Coventry: Gould, Pickering, Borrows, Rennie, Burrows, Flynn, Boland, Richardson, Ndlovu, Marsh, Dublin. Subs: Jenkinson, Pressley, Filan (gk).

Blackburn: Flowers, Berg, Hendry, Pearce, Le Saux, Ripley, Sherwood, Atkins, Warhurst, Shearer, Sutton. Subs: Newell, Slater, Mimms (gk).

Attendance: 18,547 *Points*: 73 *League Position*: 1st

Goal 32
In years to come people will talk about the slender margin of our Championship triumph and I will always think of the point we took at Coventry. We are very sloppy in the first half and lucky only to be one goal down at the interval. However, it is like the Alamo after the break as we batter away at their goal. Towards the end Coventry's defender Brian Borrows asks me if

I think I'm going to score today. I reply, 'I don't know to be honest. How long is there left?' The referee informs us there are eight minutes to go. Five minutes later I grab the equaliser. Graeme Le Saux knocks a long, hopeful ball forward and I challenge Jonathan Gould for it. It glances off my head and, despite the efforts of David Burrows, rolls into the net. I shake hands with Brian Borrows after the game and tell him, 'You should never have asked me that.' I also make a comment to the Press that this might well be the goal that clinches the Championship for us.

Saturday 18th March 1995
FA Carling Premiership

Blackburn Rovers 2	Chelsea 1
Shearer (16) Sherwood (37)	Stein (3)

Blackburn: Flowers, Berg, Hendry, Pearce, Kenna, Ripley, Sherwood, Atkins, Le Saux, Shearer, Sutton. Subs: Newell, Slater, Mimms (gk).

Chelsea: Hitchcock, Clarke, Johnsen, Sinclair, Myers, Burley, Peacock, Spackman, Rocastle, Furlong. Stein. Subs: Lee, Hall, Colgan (gk).

Attendance: 25,490 *Points*: 76 *League Position*: 1st

Goal 33 – 100th career goal (League games)
The newspapers have been mentioning for a couple of days that I need just one more to complete my century of League goals. At least it gives them something other than the Championship to write about. When the goal arrives it is a special milestone in my career. Mark Stein puts Chelsea in front so we are going flat out for an equaliser when my chance comes. Graeme Le Saux has been moved forward to play in midfield and he chips the

ball behind Erland Johnsen to leave me one-on-one with Kevin Hitchcock. The Chelsea goalkeeper stands up as long as possible and denies me a good view of the target but in the end I hit it as hard as I can and take him by surprise with the power of my shot. My ton of goals has come much more quickly than I expected, mainly because I was not that prolific at my first club Southampton. My move to Blackburn has thrust me into centre stage and given me more opportunities to grab the spotlight. I appreciate I am fortunate to play in a position where I am going to attract a lot of attention but I am first to acknowledge the contribution of my team-mates.

Saturday 1st April 1995
FA Carling Premiership

Everton 1	Blackburn Rovers 2
Stuart (24)	Sutton (1)
	Shearer (7)

Everton: Southall, Jackson, Watson, Ablett, Barrett, Hinchcliffe, Stuart, Horne, Parkinson, Amokachi, Barlow. Subs: Grant, Holmes, Kearton (gk).

Blackburn: Flowers, Berg, Pearce, Hendry, Kenna, Ripley, Sherwood, Atkins, Le Saux, Shearer, Sutton. Subs: Witschge, Newell, Mimms (gk).

Attendance: 37,905 *Points*: 79 *League Position*: 1st

Goal 34
This is a really crazy game. We go 2-0 up but come under the cosh as Everton bombard our penalty area. They deserve at least a point but it is the sort of match which makes you realise you do not always get your just rewards in football. It is that time of the season where you don't stop to analyse every performance, however. You just grab the points and run. Chris Sutton puts us

ahead with the season's fastest goal in the Premiership – after just thirteen seconds – and I add a second with a well worked free-kick move. Tim Sherwood plays the ball in, I dummy it and although Chris Sutton tries to knock it back to me, I think it is Gary Ablett who gets a slight touch. I shoot as hard as I can and, the ball finds the bottom corner of the net. Then we get our tin hats out and defend for all we are worth. I equal my best scoring run of the season in this game – four consecutive games with a goal – and it's great for my confidence at this crucial time.

Tuesday 4th April 1995
FA Carling Premiership

Queens Park Rangers 0 Blackburn Rovers 1

Sutton (68)

QPR: Roberts, Wilson, McDonald, Ready, Brevett, Sinclair, Barker, Holloway, Impey, Gallen, Ferdinand. Subs: Penrice, Dichio, Dykstra (gk).

Blackburn: Flowers, Berg, Hendry, Pearce, Le Saux, Ripley, Sherwood, Atkins, Kenna, Shearer, Sutton. Subs: Witschge, Warhurst, Mimms (gk).

Attendance: 16,508 *Points*: 82 *League Position*: 1st

Saturday 15th April 1995
FA Carling Premiership

Leeds United 1 Blackburn Rovers 1

Deane (90) Hendry (45)

Leeds: Lukic, Kelly, Wetherall, Pemberton, Dorigo, Palmer, Wallace, McAllister, Speed, Deane, Yeboah. Subs: Whelan, Worthington, Beeney (gk).

Blackburn: Flowers, Berg, Hendry, Pearce, Le Saux, Kenna, Atkins, Sherwood, Ripley, Shearer, Sutton. Subs: Batty, Gallacher, Mimms (gk).

Attendance: 39,426 *Points*: 83 *League Position*: 1st

Monday 17th April 1995
FA Carling Premiership

Blackburn Rovers 2	Manchester City 3
Shearer (7)	Curle (pen 32)
Hendry (39)	Rosler (57)
	Walsh (71)

Blackburn: Flowers, Berg, Hendry, Pearce, Le Saux, Kenna, Sherwood, Atkins, Ripley, Shearer, Sutton. Subs: Batty, Gallacher, Mimms (gk).

Manchester City: Coton, Foster, Curle, Kernaghan, Edghill, Summerbee, Flitcroft, Simpson, Walsh, Quinn, Rosler. Subs: Beagrie, D. Brightwell, Burridge (gk).

Attendance: 27,851 *Points*: 83 *League Position*: 1st

Goal 35
I score after only seven minutes with a piece of quick thinking. The conditions are terrible – a waterlogged pitch and pouring rain – and goalkeeper Tony Coton hits an attempted clearance straight to me about 25 yards from goal. It flashes through my mind in an instant: 'Why not hit it back first time?' I am rather fortunate because the ball slides past the keeper helped along by the wet surface, otherwise Coton might well have reached it. A great start but we are well beaten on the night and thoughts suddenly begin to emerge that the title is slipping away from us.

Thursday 20th April 1995
FA Carling Premiership

Blackburn Rovers 2 — Crystal Palace 1

Kenna (47) — Houghton (71)
Gallacher (51)

Blackburn: Flowers, Kenna, Berg, Pearce, Le Saux, Ripley, Atkins, Batty, Gallacher, Shearer, Sutton. Subs: Newell, Slater, Mimms (gk).

Crystal Palace: Wilmot, Patterson, Shaw, Young, Coleman, Gordon, Houghton, Southgate, Newman, Dowie, Armstrong. Subs: Humphrey, Cox, Glass (gk).

Attendance: 28,005 *Points*: 86 *League Position*: 1st

Sunday 30th April 1995
FA Carling Premiership

West Ham United 2 — Blackburn Rovers 0

Rieper (51)
Hutchison (83)

West Ham: Miklosko, Breacker, Rieper, Potts, Dicks, Allen, Bishop, Moncur, Holmes, Boere, Hutchison. Subs: Rush, Webster, Sealey (gk).

Blackburn: Flowers, Kenna, Berg, Hendry, Le Saux, Ripley, Sherwood, Batty, Witschge, Shearer, Sutton. Subs: Newell, Atkins, Mimms (gk).

Attendance: 24,202 *Points*: 86 *League Position*: 1st

Monday 8th May 1995
FA Carling Premiership

Blackburn Rovers 1 Newcastle United 0

Shearer (29)

Blackburn: Flowers, Berg, Hendry, Pearce, Kenna, Ripley, Sherwood, Batty, Le Saux, Shearer, Sutton. Subs: Newell, Slater, Mimms (gk).

Newcastle: Srnicek, Hottiger, Peacock, Howey, Beresford, Gillespie, Clark, Watson, Fox, Beardsley, Lee. Subs: Neilson, Allen, Hooper (gk).

Attendance: 30,545 *Points*: 89 *League Position*: 1st

Goal 36
Few goals give me as much of a thrill as this one. We cannot settle for anything other than a victory because the situation at the top is so tight. My family and friends are out in force again as we face my second favourite club. After about half an hour Graeme Le Saux takes the ball to the by-line and chips it over the head of the keeper. I am running in at the far post and that gives me a distinct advantage over defender John Beresford who is standing still. I climb above him and head the ball down into the net. I have never known such an atmosphere at Ewood Park. Nor have I felt such tension. Newcastle over-run us in the second half but Tim Flowers beats them back with the best goalkeeping display I have ever seen.

Sunday 14th May 1995
FA Carling Premiership

Liverpool 2 Blackburn Rovers 1

Barnes (64) Shearer (20)
Redknapp (90)

Attendance: 40,014 *Points*: 89 *League Position*: 1st – Champions

Liverpool: James, Thomas, Scales, Harkness, Babb, McManaman, Barnes, Redknapp, Kennedy, Fowler, Clough. Subs: Walters, Matteo, Warner (gk).

Blackburn: Flowers, Berg, Pearce, Hendry, Le Saux, Ripley, Sherwood, Batty, Kenna, Shearer, Sutton. Subs: Newell, Slater, Mimms (gk).

Goal 37
The last day of the season brings a strange mixture of emotions from total despair to confusion and then to ecstasy. My 37th goal of the season in all competitions gives us the lead. I play the ball out to Stuart Ripley on the right-hand side and, as he pulls it back, I have to slow down to take the ball in my stride. I think the ball goes through John Scales' legs before beating David James. When the ball hits the back of the net, I remember thinking, 'Just go crazy. Just go wild.' But I manage to see sense and keep calm when I realise there is still a long way to go. My goal is soon forgotten as the events of the day unfold. Liverpool win with goals from John Barnes and Jamie Redknapp but Manchester United are held by West Ham. What a day. What a climax. What a season.

APPEARANCES AND GOAL-SCORERS

1994/95

APPEARANCES

PLAYER	PREMIER LEAGUE	COCA-COLA CUP	FA CUP	UEFA CUP	CHARITY SHIELD	SEASON TOTAL
Shearer	42	3	2	2		49
Berg	40	4	2	2	1	49
Sutton	40	4	2	2		48
Flowers	39	4	2	2	1	48
Le Saux	39	4	2	2	1	48
Hendry	38	4	2	2	1	47
Sherwood	38	3	1	2	1	45
Ripley	36 (1)	4	1	2	1	44 (1)
Atkins	30 (4)	3	2	1 (1)	1	37 (5)
Wilcox	27	4	2	2	1	36
Warhurst	20 (7)	4	2	0 (1)		26 (8)
Pearce	22 (6)	0 (1)	1	0 (1)	1	24 (8)
Gale	15	2	0	2	1	20
Slater	12 (6)	1	1	1	1	16 (6)
Kenna	8	0	0	0	0	8
Wright	4 (1)	0	0 (1)	0	0	4 (2)
Batty	4 (1)	0	0	0	0	4 (1)
Mimms	3 (1)	0	0	0	0	3 (1)
Newell	2 (10)	0 (1)	0 (2)	0	0	2 (13)
Gallacher	1	0	0	0	0	1
Witschge	1	0	0	0	0	1

PLAYER	PREMIER LEAGUE	COCA-COLA CUP	FA CUP	UEFA CUP	CHARITY SHIELD	SEASON TOTAL
Makel	0	0	0 (1)	0	0	0 (1)
Thorne	0	0	0	0	0 (1)	0 (1)

(Sub appearances in brackets.)

51 Games: 42 Premiership, 4 Coca-Cola Cup, 2 FA Cup, 2 UEFA Cup, 1 Charity Shield.

GOAL-SCORERS

PLAYER	PREMIER LEAGUE	COCA-COLA CUP	FA CUP	UEFA CUP	TOTAL
Shearer	34	2	0	1	37
Sutton	15	3	2	1	21
Sherwood	6	0	0	0	6
Atkins	6	0	0	0	6
Wilcox	5	1	0	0	6
Hendry	4	0	0	0	4
Le Saux	3	0	0	0	3
Warhurst	2	0	0	0	2
Berg	1	0	0	0	1
Kenna	1	0	0	0	1
Gallacher	1	0	0	0	1
Own goals	2	0	0	0	1